AF505867

Lucian Freud

A CLOSER LOOK

Contents

Lucian Freud

A CLOSER LOOK

WORKS FROM THE UBS ART COLLECTION

LOUISIANA MUSEUM OF MODERN ART

Preface

Creating exhibitions from the UBS Art Collection offers many unique and wonderful opportunities. With many thousands of works of art from around the world to choose from, whether they are American Pop Art masterworks or pieces by the newest and most dynamic artists from Asia and Latin America, the public exhibitions from the collection that I have had the privilege to work on in recent years have been focused on bringing the work of many artists together under unifying subjects and themes, emphasising the breadth and geographic spread of the whole collection, and making use of the long and diverse nature of its continuing creation. By contrast, this exhibition is a rare opportunity to look at one of the collection's moments of extraordinary depth, as well as the influence of one individual on an important aspect of its character.

The opportunity to have a significant museum exhibition from the UBS Art Collection which consists of the work of a single artist owes its existence to two exceptional elements: the long history of Donald B. Marron's leadership of a key part of the collection, and the more recent connection between UBS and our friends and partners at the Louisiana Museum of Modern Art. The legacy at UBS of former board member Donald Marron and his involvement in the development of the art collection are profoundly evident, but nowhere more so than in the exceptional group of works by Lucian Freud which he acquired for the firm over many years of conscientious collecting, resulting in a group of prints that represents the vast majority of the artist's works in that medium, as well as some stunning unique works. The recognition of this group by Anders Kold and Poul Erik Tøjner at the Louisiana as worthy of forming the core of this exhibition is a great privilege, and with their addition of a smaller group of rare and important prints from another collection, we have an even more welcome opportunity to share a treasured part of the UBS Art Collection with the world, through one of its most intriguing and influential art institutions.

Stephen McCoubrey
Regional Curator for Europe and Asia, UBS Art Collection

Foreword

The exhibition *Lucian Freud – A Closer Look* is a wonderful chance to get close to an artist's work. 'A Closer Look' is moreover what Louisiana's series *Louisiana on Paper*, supported over the years by The David Foundation, is all about – intimacy, small formats; reading instead of scanning, plumbing the depths of the individual work and its variations instead of allowing oneself to be overawed by the gestures of the big exhibitions. Add to this finally that *Lucian Freud – A Closer Look* – as an intensive special study – comes in the wake of Louisiana's acquisition of the print *Woman with an Arm Tattoo*, 1996, a gift from the Ny Carlsberg Foundation in 2002, and after the major presentation of the painter Freud in 2007, it could hardly be better for a museum.

That it has gone so well is due to the collaboration between Louisiana and UBS, from whose collection the overwhelming majority of the works shown have been taken. A further ten trial proof etchings have been added to the exhibition by kind intermission by Graham Southern of Blain|Southern, London.

The UBS Art Collection is a unique collection and I would like to express my gratitude to UBS, which for the past year has been the sponsor of Louisiana Learning in Humlebæk. Special thanks to the curator Stephen McCoubrey, UBS Art Collection, Søren Kjær, Managing Director, UBS WM Nordics, and Annabelle von Trott, Marketing UBS WM Europe, for their dedicated commitment to the exhibition and the drawing-up of this catalogue.

Poul Erik Tøjner
Director, Louisiana Museum of Modern Art

Freud's Man and Beast

Anders Kold

Anders Kold

You can't be aware enough. I've always thought that biology was a great help to me and perhaps even having worked with animals was a help. I thought through observation I could make something into my own that might not have been seen or noticed in that way before.[1]

This will be all about seeing: about taking a closer look at the English artist Lucian Freud's prints. In his own words, there is hardly any limit to how much effort one must make as an artist – and that applies to the whole field of subjects: human beings, animals and objects. Being able to make something into one's own, as he puts it, means in Freud's case, among other things, privileging art and the artwork as a self-sufficient entity more than any other. The other implications of the subject – environment, geography, era, social relations and whatever else we think of when looking at another creature – are either secondary or quite absent.

What we in fact see and sense, we who look at the works beyond the control exercised by the artist's gaze and framing, is another matter. For Freud it is his truth about the seen – often the result of a hard struggle, one feels – that is held forth. Choices and adaptations which a photograph, for example, cannot offer. This hard-won truth – the intensified observation, drained of less central circumstantiality – has often been characterized as the *essence* of the subject. There is a long-standing tradition within modernity in support of this interpretative practice, as there also is for a closely related crisis of representation. A classic example, and one with intimate connections with

The Egyptian Book. 1994. Cat. 37

Louisiana's historic collection, is the painter and sculptor Alberto Giacometti. In the 1930s, when he was attacked in the Surrealist circles in Paris for taking up life-drawing again – after all, everyone knows what a head looks like – his reply was that "no one has ever really looked at a face before".

For Freud and many of his contemporaries, however, the challenge of taking a closer look was clear and meaningful, also in the cases, by no means rare, when the post-war avant-gardes took art in other directions and outside Great Britain, where biology, as represented by the animals Freud mentions, has always maintained a rather robust grip on the world-picture and the senses.

Nevertheless Freud was not born in the green and pleasant isle, but in Berlin. He came to England as a ten-year-old Jewish immigrant in 1933, the year of the Nazi seizure of power and the dissolution of the high culture and tradition of knowledge that the country of his birth had represented. The etching *The Egyptian Book* (cat. 37) is a central work that not only associates the country of his childhood with the new one, but also reveals quite central aspects of Freud's art. It is based on a double-page opening with two photographic plates in the Egyptologist J.H. Breasted's *Geschichte Ägyptens* from 1936. Freud received the book as a gift in England at the beginning of the war, and it must have stood for him as a dreamtrack linking a remote and recent past – ancient Egypt and

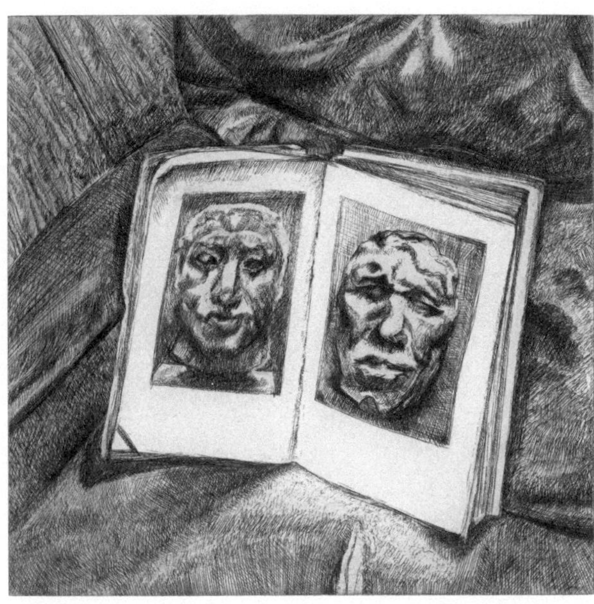

Germany. The sculptures in the two black-and-white reproductions of Egyptian pharaohs were in the museum in Berlin, and with their half-closed and seemingly inward-gazing eyes share the fate of many of Freud's living models. In Freud's interpretation the strange thing that happens in the etching is that the two ancient rulers in the worn book become human again, so to speak, and appear more alive than some of his living models. Twice the artist has painted the subject, but it is in the etching, where line is substituted for brush stroke and creates a heightened awareness of structure and sculptural effect, that Freud's vision is most affecting. He appears to have looked at them at very close quarters. He himself says somewhere: "I thought about those people a lot. There's nothing like them: they're human before Egyptian in a way".[2] In the lines of the etchings they are dragged into the present, as William Feaver points out: "They are whoever they are, irrespective of context, not mere relics or illustrations".[3] If one were to push the concept to the limits, one could say that they have just left their position *sub specie aeternitatis* to take up a new one in the space of art and the artist in a way that does not differ substantially from Freud's living models.

The model for the work *Woman with an Arm Tattoo* (cat. 53) may be of flesh and blood; but she is depicted by the artist with no consideration of what her milieu or immediate situation might otherwise be. In Freud's works there is no surrounding world, no sociality and no space in which to act. And whether one comes to think of butterflies mounted on pins or Madame Cézanne's statement that she was simply an orange in her husband's still lifes, it is clear that Freud controls everything in the works with a wilful determination. The woman is asleep, which aligns her with a multitude of other naked people whose contact with the world around them is defined by side-

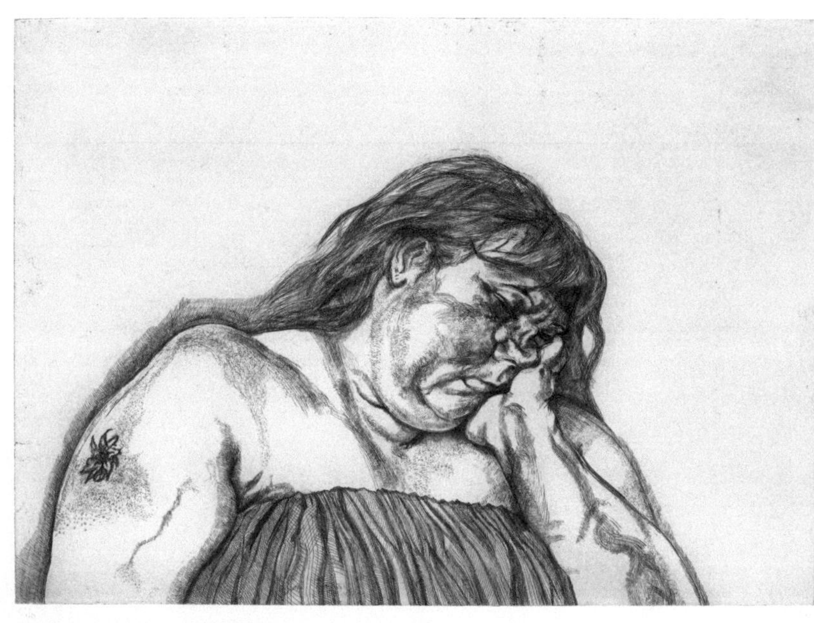

Woman with an Arm Tattoo. 1996. Cat. 53

After Chardin (large plate). 2000. Cat. 58

long, casual, veiled and shifty gazes – and in this case sleep; an introversion and absorption that explains Freud's preoccupation with Jean-Siméon Chardin's painting *The Young Schoolmistress*, which conveniently hung just around the corner from Freud, in the National Gallery in London. It shows two figures intensely absorbed in their tasks and unaware of the world around them.

Freud's *After Chardin* (large plate) and the somewhat smaller *After Chardin* (small plate) (cat. 58 & 59), which show only the schoolmistress's profile and the area around her ear and her hairline in particular, moves in only one direction: inward and away from us. At the same time we can dwell here on a classic example of Freud's pronounced interest in the sensory organs and other ducts, including the genitals, in humans and animals. Looking closely at the tattooed woman, one will see that the area around eyes, nose and mouth, in its relaxed state, is rendered like a patch of war-wound surgery, a momentarily indefinable sculptural lump. This radical concern with the physicality of the body should not mislead us, however, into thinking that the artist did any old thing with nature in the service of the picture. Other works exist, both paintings and prints, of the same woman, and in several of them Freud has left out the tattoo on the arm – left out, for as Freud himself said: "I feel it is immoral to put anything in that isn't there. But it is not necessarily immoral to leave out something that is there".[4]

As a further, if subtle example of the reciprocity in Freud's work between observed life and its representations in art – and with those pharaohs in mind – one can imagine Freud enjoying this little marker of civilization and the image-making urge as it draws attention to itself amidst the overwhelming physique.

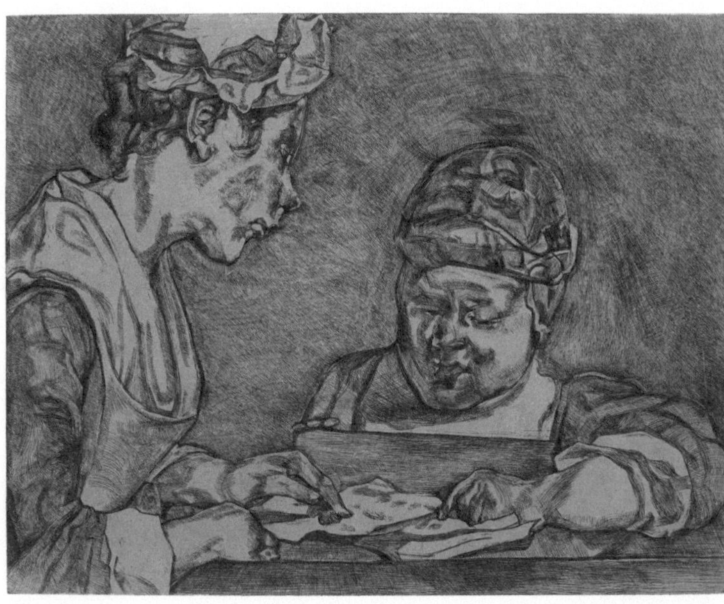

There is good reason to believe that the dog and the woman in the etching *Pluto* (cat. 25) are identical to those seen in the slightly later painting *Double Portrait* (cat. 63). The etching is most certainly not a double portrait – if it is at all compatible with the genre, it is of course Pluto, the dog, that is portrayed. But the state of the picture only arose in a late phase when Freud's colleague, Frank Auerbach, urged the artist to remove something from the top and thus cut the woman's face out of the original subject. From this we can infer two things: that nothing is sacred with respect to the pictorial truth, and that in his art Freud often does not meet the genre criteria normally used by art history. It is presumably the case with many of the great authors that they do not see the whole course of a novel laid out in front of them before the work begins. Or ends. Process and artistic freedom are paramount. So too with Freud, but unlike the author Freud can cut through, irrespective of milieu and period, to the individual as a unique occurrence in the world.

The second factor, Freud's sometimes radical motivic slippages between portraiture, still life and genre picture, brings us to something that touches on the above-mentioned absorption. In *Pluto* the whole action is turned in towards the work itself. If Freud had subscribed to the notions of the avant-garde, the work would have been derived, as was the case with his colleague Francis Bacon, from a fondness for the fragment and an active awareness of the great aesthetic innovation of modernity, the photograph, and then of the moving images of the film. But Freud did not.

With infinite sophistication the cropping leaves the bodies hanging in the framing vacuum that Freud so often favoured. All else has gone – and something of the duo in the picture with it. This makes the bodily relationship the true subject – uncut, so to speak. Not a genre-specific motif, but an accurate record of something seen. Something, that is, seen anew, after the cropping of the original state, which brings out the autonomous points of the artwork: in a way, forcing the figures into the picture space and through this scaling also changes the angle of gaze. This is a device that testifies to the bodily experience of the subject that Freud exploits and insists on. No other requirement is to be honoured. Man and beast can thus look as vacuum-packed as one likes in their de-aerated space.

Portrait commissions set limits to how far from the world – and thus from the viewer – a person can be. And portraits made up a not insignificant part of Freud's oeuvre. There is no shortage of descriptions of how he approached the work, nor of the merciless control he is said to have exerted over his models. That a power game was involved in the process – portrait or not – is obvious. Everything seems to be entirely in his hands, with precision and consistency. *Lord Goodman in His Yellow Pyjamas* (cat. 21)*,* though, is an example of a person who is giving nothing away. In fact it could be a picture of the artist, insistently considering his subject. This is world-class portraiture – at a time, into the bargain, when the genre can only haltingly keep up with art's other incursions and excursions.

Pluto. 1988. Cat. 25

In the end we must ask ourselves what it is we see and sense when we look at Freud's works. Whether his radical observational powers, despite everything, in fact reach out to us and activate something other than just *his* angle and the sense of sharing a look under the skin of the models. Freud's works also challenge us for other reasons. Do we not in reality also see ourselves each time we look at Freud's works? Bodily sensations are aroused in the viewer as memory of one's own body and psyche. Arrogantly staring or with shifty gaze. Or sleeping with all the loss of control that frequently entails, and often forced into daunting non-idealized glimpses of our mortal frames. Not as human specimens disinterestedly viewed, for along the way Freud too has felt something and in the process has incorporated in his works fragments of conversation, moods and reactions from the genesis of the works. We are left, in other words, even when the space and the social ambience of the artwork have been excised, and the genre conventions have only partially been fulfilled, with more than, or perhaps rather something other than the *essence*. This inconclusiveness is a productive and legitimate feeling in an art museum.[5]

1. William Feaver: *Lucian Freud: Life into Art,* Tate Publishing 2002, p. 40. **2**. Op. cit., p. 14. **3**. Loc. cit. **4**. Robert Hughes: *Lucian Freud Paintings,* The British Council, London 1987, p. 19. **5**. Poul Erik Tøjner: "Forord" in *Louisiana Revy,* vol. 48 no. 1, 2007, p. 5.

Anders Kold (b. 1959), MA in Art History from University of Copenhagen. Curator and Head of Acquisitions at Louisiana Museum of Modern Art since 2001. Organized the museum's exhibitions on a.o. Louise Bourgeois, David Hockney, Anselm Kiefer, Wolfgang Tillmans, Thomas Demand, Tal R, Doug Aitken, Jorn & Pollock and Jeff Wall. Anders Kold is the author of a number of essays, introductions and magazine articles on art and contemporary culture.

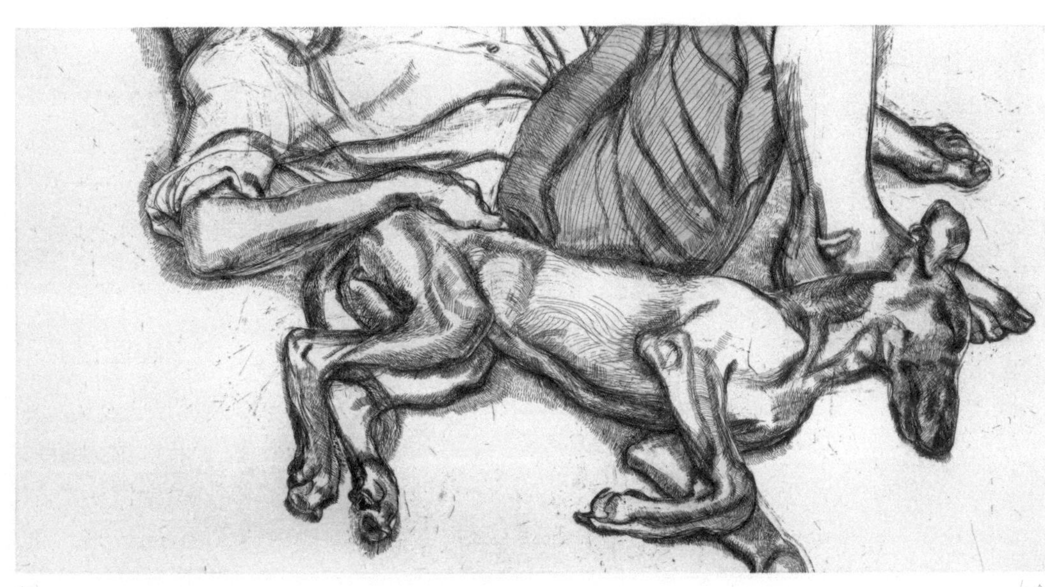

Lucian Freud: The Trenchant Gaze

Richard Cork

Ever since he died in 2011, Lucian Freud's reputation as an artist has been dominated by the dramatically surging prices which his work commands at auction. It is a shame, because art-market speculation distracts our attention from the true reason why Freud is worth remembering. He was, without any doubt, one of the most intense figurative painters of the modern period — an incisive observer of the people who came to his London house in Kensington Church Street, rang the bell and found themselves admitted to his remarkable studio on the first floor.

I will never forget being taken up there by Freud. The studio was long and luminous. In one corner of the room, the walls were covered with a hailstorm of brushmarks. Below them, a paint-smeared table filled with artist's materials stood ready to be used. Nearby, an easel supported a recently finished painting. "I never pose anyone", Freud told me. "They move around and I say: 'will you relax a bit more?'". In this instance, the woman lay on the bed and, according to Freud, "slept very easily. But no position is that comfortable." Especially when a single painting session could last up to six or seven hours. He showed me the bed in the other half of the studio, wrily explaining that his insistence on standing while he painted for such extended periods "makes my back and neck get sore."

The sustained intensity of his looking, however, bore mesmerising fruit in the paintings he produced. Take *Double Portrait* (cat. 63), a large canvas executed over a long period at the end of the 1980s and the beginning of the following decade.

Double Portrait. 1988–90. Cat. 63

Looking at this powerful work, we might at first imagine that both woman and dog are essentially relaxed. After all, she has decided to stretch herself out on the bed, and her canine companion rests his head against her arm. The dog seems sleepy, lying as close as possible to the woman. She touches his back, and they are clearly prepared to remain together for the lengthy sessions which Freud so often demanded when he became fully engrossed in the act of painting.

But the longer we stare at this image, the more uneasy it appears. Although the woman is touching the dog, her hand is still rigid and folded tightly like a fist. She thrusts her other hand behind her head, as if determined to prevent herself from enjoying the softness of the pillow. Her legs look trapped inside the tightness of her skirt, and she seems absorbed in sombre thoughts. Then we realise that the dog's claws are disturbingly visible, suggesting that he is ready at any moment to defend himself against a possible attack.

The fact that this painting is called *Double Portrait* proves how much importance Freud attached to the presence of the animal as well as the woman. I remember noticing, on my visits to his house, that Freud's dog lay in her corner basket, next to a table where Rodin's bronze figure of Balzac asserted his full-length virility. The

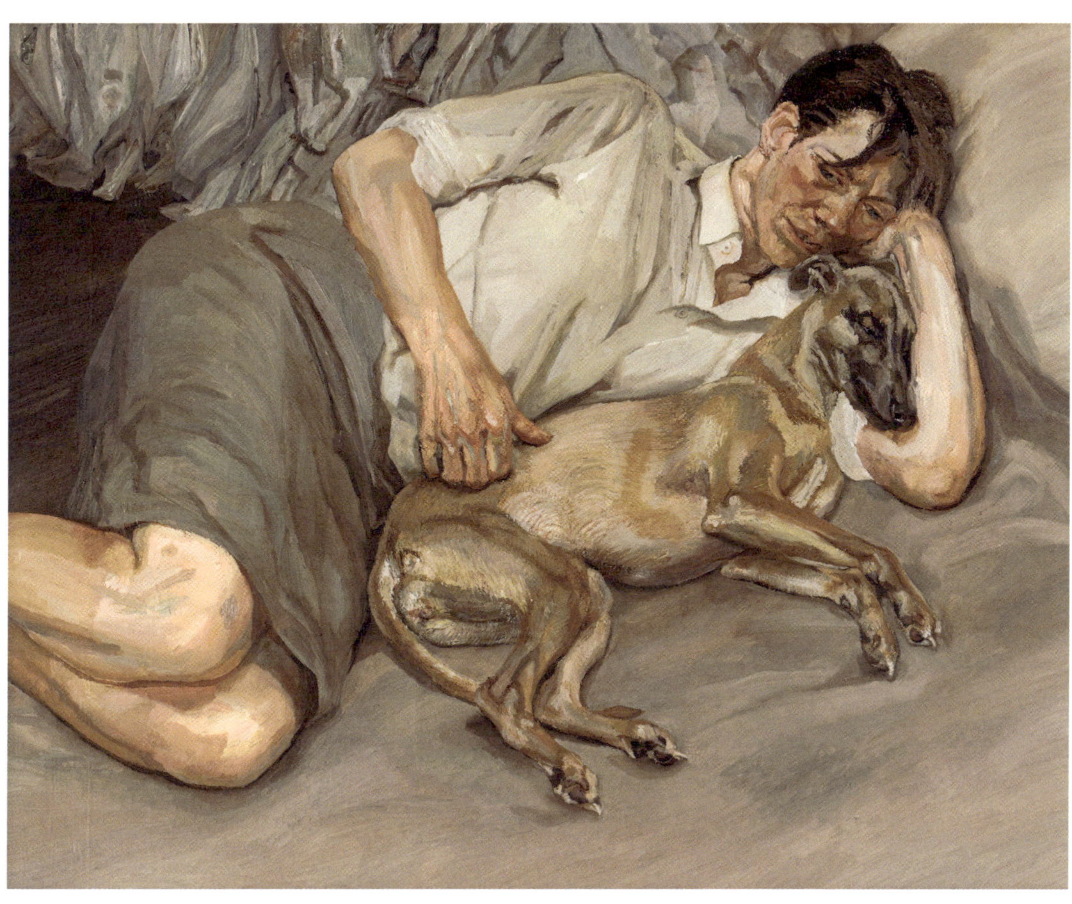

dog's lean agility reflected Freud's own astonishing energy. Even in old age, when his face became gaunt, he was still able to dart around the living room or leap upstairs with prodigious speed. His formidable dynamism and intelligence were undimmed, and Freud would work just as well during the night as he did in the daytime.

Maybe he wanted to emulate the prowess of racing animals. I recall that once, during a visit to his house, he suddenly asked me whether I would mind if we went downstairs and watched the Grand National on television. It is Britain's most important horse-racing event, and Freud had discovered his own love of riding when he was still a schoolboy. Now, in the low-ceilinged basement room which contained his TV set, he seemed very eager for the Grand National to begin, draping his legs over a chair at expectant angles while his long, thin scarf hung down from his neck to the floor. Once the race began, he grew more and more excited, telling me that

"I had a filly once — Jacob Rothschild used to look after it for me in the country, and I'd go down there to ride." He had two favourites in today's race, and one of them became the leader. "You must be delighted, Lucian", I said. "No," came the vehement reply. "If he wins, I'll be furious that I didn't actually place any bets this year!". He became more and more agitated as the favourite stormed towards the finish, but in the end — to Freud's intense relief — the horse was overtaken by a contender he did not know.

Although the UBS collection does contain another oil painting by Freud, *Head of a Naked Girl* (cat. 64) executed in 1999, the main emphasis is on his etchings. He was fascinated by this medium even at an early stage in his career, and *Head on a Pillow* (cat. 8), an etching made in 1982, is remarkably similar in subject to his 1948 etching called *Ill in Paris*. Both these works concentrate on a woman's head resting in bed. But the earlier one finds room for a flower rising up beside the pillow. The woman's large left eye is

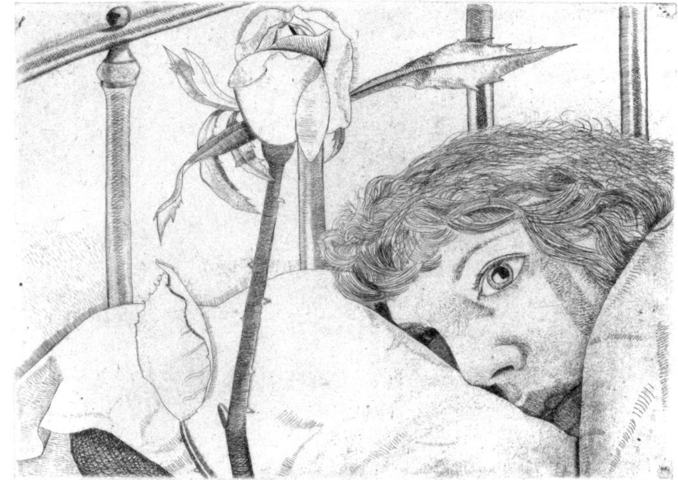

Ill in Paris. 1948

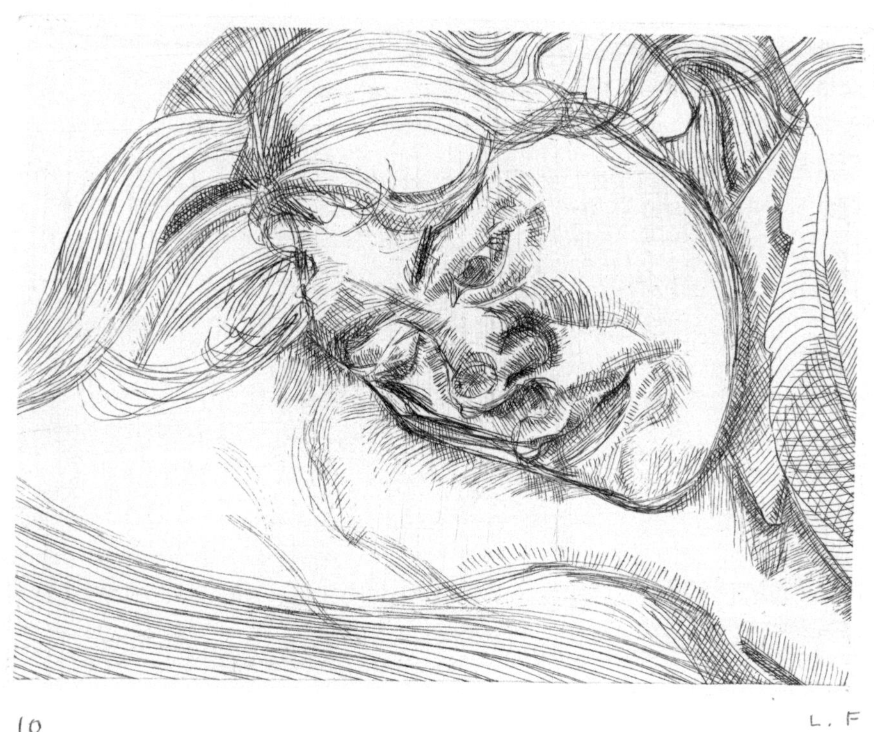

Head on a Pillow. 1982. Cat. 8

focused on the petals, and she doubtless gains a lot of pleasure from the flower's beauty. It must provide great comfort at a time when illness confines her to bed. In this respect, she is far luckier than the woman in *Head on a Pillow*. Here, Freud focuses very tightly on her face, and she gazes down at the linen rather than staring out at the world beyond. This etching is handled with far greater freedom than its predecessor in 1948. The vigorously manipulated lines emphasise the restlessness felt by this woman as she slumps on the bed. Haunted rather than serene, her face derives scant relief from lying down to rest. Paradoxically, the act of reclining seems to deepen her sense of disquiet rather than alleviating it in any way at all.

Sometimes, Freud enjoyed experimenting with adding pastel colours to his etching. A dramatic example is *Cerith* (cat. 26) in 1989, where the sitter's face threatens to burst out of the confines of the picture altogether. Freud uses his pastel to give Cerith additional bulk. He ends up possessing an almost sculptural solidity, and the combination of flesh and bone has a tactile strength. His vigour makes us feel that, any second now, he might swing his head in an entirely different direction. But for the moment, at least, he remains still and allows Freud to capture the essential weight of Cerith's monumental features.

For the most part, though, Freud preferred to concentrate on etching without adding any pastel. He was a master draughtsman, and this collection contains a remarkable cluster of the portraits he made of his daughter Bella. They are all focused on her alone. He knows her well, yet

never allows the mood to lighten. The earliest one, a 1982 etching, shows her in a reclining position. Concentrating on her head, Freud reveals a sense of latent toughness in his daughter's face. His handling is almost rough in this modest-sized image, which must have been executed far more quickly than the *Double Portrait* painting. But alongside his disclosure of her inner strength, Freud also reveals a feeling of fatigue in Bella. She looks ready to rely on the support given by the cushion. Dark shadows under her eyes intensify this mood, and Bella's eyes appear to be mesmerised by a disquieting vision.

In a larger etching produced five years later, Bella seems more resolute. This time, her head fills most of the picture-space. The collar tightly encircling her neck adds to the spirit of determination, even if it also looks somewhat restrictive. She has the air of someone bent on maintaining her privacy, although Freud is still subjecting her to his most trenchant gaze. Bella's chin appears almost pugnacious, as if reacting in a defensive manner to the artist as he moves in for a close-up view.

By the time Freud made his etching of *Bella in Her Pluto T-Shirt* (cat. 49), this tension had been replaced by a more informal alternative. Mischievous humour is evident at once: the eager Pluto is seen in tongue-wagging outline on Bella's chest, and she cocks her eyebrow perhaps to acknowledge this comic-book naughtiness. Ostensibly at ease in the summer T-shirt, she allows her mouth to suggest the beginnings of a smile. Freud enjoys framing her figure within the sculptural structure of a wicker chair, which gives the entire composition an imposing presence. At the same time, though, the mood of this etching is laced with a profound feeling of mystery. Bella, propping her head against another bunched-up hand, may well be pondering on the strangeness inherent in submitting herself to Freud's scrutiny. She could even be wondering why her father is always so committed to the rigour of this self-imposed task, which absorbs most of his energy and makes him return, with obsessive discipline, to the daily challenge of defining human figures.

Like his eminent grandfather Sigmund before him, Lucian never stopped inviting men, women and children to enter his sanctum. Yet unlike the pioneering psychoanalyst, Lucian positioned them in bare rooms unalleviated by the rugs, drapes and rows of companionable statuettes which lined Sigmund's consulting rooms in Vienna and London alike. There is no suggestion that the people in Lucian's paintings and etchings suffer from the mental turmoil afflicting his grandfather's clients. But the faces in this extensive collection of Freud's work are far from blithe. Apart from *Bella in Her Pluto T-Shirt*, nobody smiles. One woman, simply called Susanna, seems to raise her fist in an attempt to hide some vestige of herself from the artist's avid stare. Most of them, though, accept the inevitability of exposure. Because they have posed for him before, they know that Freud will subject their flesh to an almost clinical examination. And he sees them, above all, as solitary. Nothing can deflect him from a constant desire to explore their underlying isolation.

In this respect, Freud's mature vision was still informed by memories of his own early life. As a boy, he had experienced a sudden, irreversible uprooting. Determined to escape the Nazis in 1933, his beleaguered family moved to London from his native Berlin. And even in the final phase of his long career, Freud's work still seemed to reflect this childhood sense of dislocation. "My work is purely autobiographical", he once declared. "It is about myself and my surroundings. It is an attempt at a record. I work from the people that interest me, and that I care about and think about, in rooms that I live in and know. I use the people to invent my pictures with, and I can work more freely when they are there."

Knowing that Freud spent his boyhood years in Berlin, many writers have been eager to detect in his early work the influence of the most searching German artists of that time. But while he must have been affected by growing up in the feverish atmosphere of the Weimar Republic, it is too easy to suggest that he derived his artistic stimulus from such sources alone. Cedric Morris, his first art teacher in England, proved just as influential. When the 18-year-old Freud painted Morris in 1940, his admiration for the teacher's own art was clear. The link between them is inescapable, yet Freud would later learn how to replace this roughly summarised approach to portraiture with a more penetrating, minutely-observed alternative. None of his works in the present exhibition is early enough in date to reveal his preoccupation with closely observed detail. It reached an unforgettable climax in Freud's small 1952 portrait of Francis Bacon, who was his friend for many years.

Freud subsequently moved away from minutiae in favour of a broader approach. He proved that, in an age of avant-garde abstraction, there were still ways of revitalising the figurative tradition. During the final decades of his life, Freud came to be ranked among the finest painters at work anywhere in the world, and the images collected by UBS add up to a compelling demonstration of his later achievements. Many of them focus on women's heads, and prove that he has never been afraid to reveal sagging flesh, wrinkles, blotches and all the other marks that distinguish real female faces from their ever more glamourised and titillating counterparts in fashionable, idealised imagery.

His 1982 etching of *The Painter's Mother* (cat. 10) is utterly uncompromising. With mouth firmly closed, the elderly matriarch frowns as she stares into space. The intensity of her eyes is startling — she might easily be recalling some incident from pre-war Berlin life that continues to haunt her. Freud's mother sat for him on many occasions in her later years. Bereaved and lonely, she no doubt derived comfort from his presence. But Freud does not allow *The Painter's Mother* to be compromised by any kind of sentimental complacency. Far from it: the pain in her furrowed features is emphasised rather than softened. The etching needle has been harshly deployed, by an artist set on arriving above all at pictorial truth.

Freud's commitment to honesty was admirable, and it did not prevent him from taking risks. Look at his etching of the writer, curator and artist Lawrence Gowing (cat. 9). Although executed in the same year as *The Painter's Mother*, it could hardly be more different. Instead of gazing outwards, Gowing looks down. The hair remaining on his scalp has been flattened, so that it appears more controlled than the wilder hair sprouting from the mother's head. Gowing, too,

   The Painter's Mother. 1982. Cat. 10

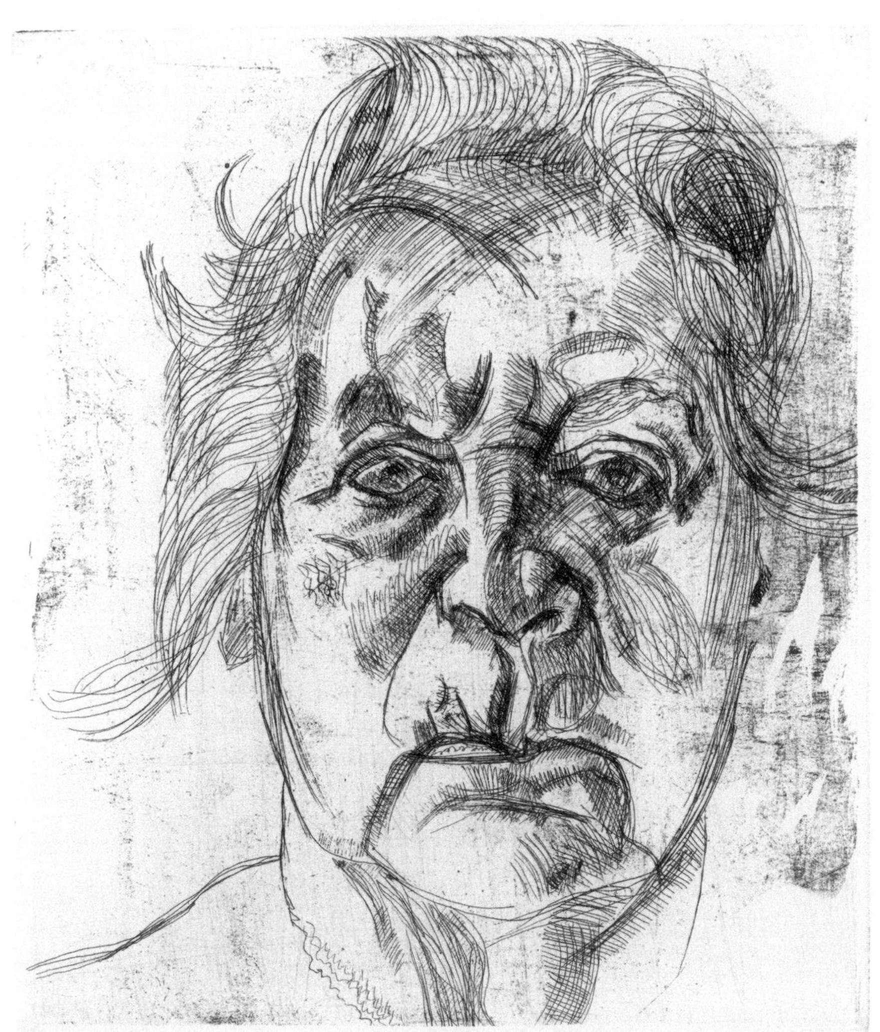

A/P. VII/X   L. F.

is confronting the inevitability of old age. Yet he seems to accept it in a more philosophical way. Far from feeling shocked by some traumatic memory, he may well be lost in contemplation of the great painters he wrote about with such distinction. Freud shades Gowing's features, so that they almost disappear into darkness. The contrast with *The Painter's Mother* is extreme, making us realise just how dramatically Freud seems to have trained a searchlight on her features and emphasised their defiant resilience.

No amount of innate vitality could prevent Leigh Bowery from succumbing to AIDS-related illness. Freud painted and drew him a great deal in the final years of his life, and the two images in the collection appear initially to stress Bowery's robustness. *Head of a Man* (cat. 20), the smaller and earlier of them, zooms in on his mighty head. Bowery's baldness emphasises the immensity of his skull, and Freud isolates a circle of glistening light near the apex. But he also allows ominous shadows to dance across his sitter's skin. Bowery's expression is gravely stoical. He appears to be accepting the prospect of death rather than allowing it to make him distraught.

His nakedness accentuates this vulnerability, and the surrounding darkness seems about to invade him.

Hindsight, of course, affects our response to these etched portraits of Bowery. The second one, considerably bigger and produced a year later, is far more monumental. Freud simply calls it *Large Head* (cat. 36), and makes us aware of the strength in his sitter's left shoulder, thrusting out of the space. Bowery appears to have lost some of the weight which made *Head of a Man* a more sedate image. We might even be tempted to think that he looks healthier in *Large Head*, and Freud gives Bowery the forcefulness of a carving as he dominates a space far lighter than the shadowy interior in *Head of a Man*. Now the skull looks chiselled, its hardness contrasting with the plump flesh still amply gathered under his chin. Despite Bowery's immense presence and dignity, we feel the sadness of a man who must have felt old before his time. Freud clearly wants his friend to overcome illness and survive. At the same time, though, *Large Head* is riddled with intimations of mortality. The longer we look at it, the more resigned Bowery seems to his own inescapable, untimely extinction.

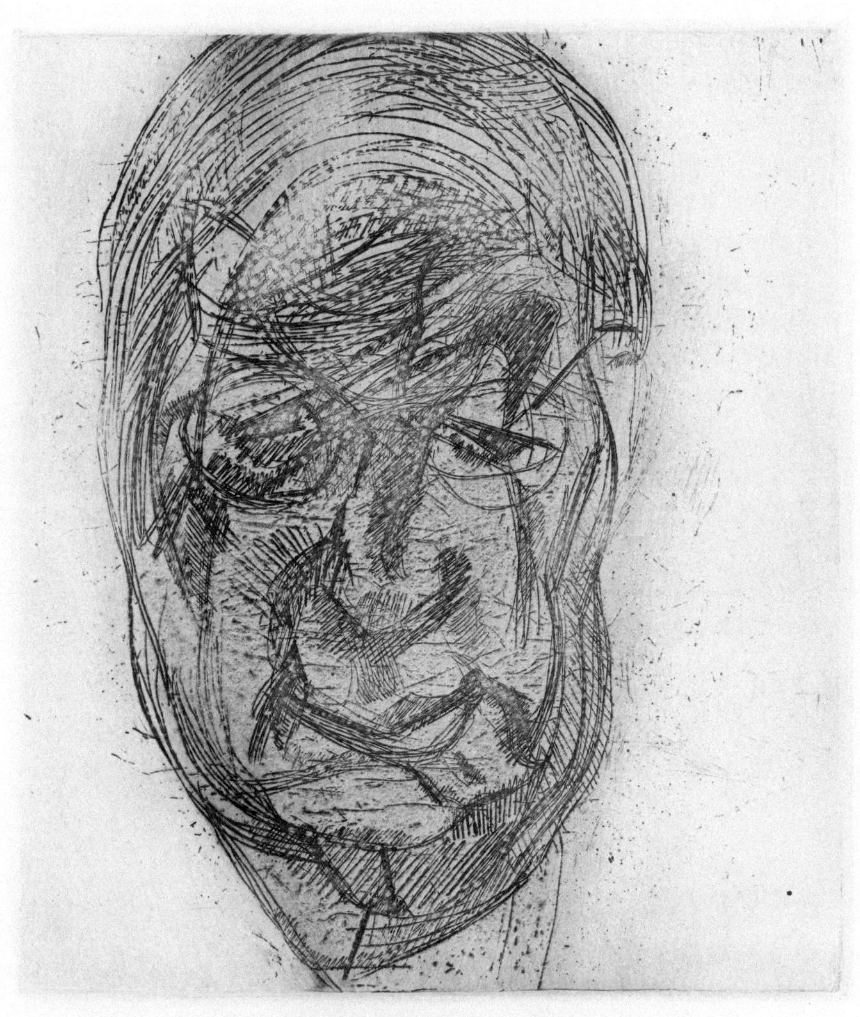

2/10

L,F

Bowery is also the subject of *Reclining Figure* (cat. 48), and the Louisiana exhibition has been fortunate enough to borrow from another London collection an arresting series of prints showing how Freud worked through dramatically different states of this single etching (cat. 38-47). Bowery is seen from above in the first state, naked and resting his head on his hand. Unusually in Freud's work, we can hardly see the face. The centre of the etching is dominated by the top of Bowery's head, and Freud then reworked it with pastel additions. The result is somewhat ghostly, and he felt so dissatisfied that the head was erased. But extensive additions followed, so the etching's second state replaced this eerie absence with a more reassuring alternative. Freud, however, was still unhappy. He now made chalk additions, particularly to Bowery's forehead and nose. Then, the chalk alternatives were themselves removed. By the time Freud arrived at the third state, Bowery's nose had been redefined and placed in a higher position. Yet even now Freud could not leave *Reclining Figure* alone. The third state was reprinted on off-white paper, but then he cancelled it with fierce diagonal lines scratched across Bowery's head, arms and hands. Looking at this alarmingly destructive proof almost makes us feel we are witnessing the moment when he died.

Even so, by no means all the etchings exhibited at Louisiana make us think about mortality. The woman in *Head and Shoulders* (cat. 4) may look somewhat tousled as she bares her flesh and submits to Freud's piercing inspection, but he celebrates her stamina and resolve, as well as emphasising the robustness of the ample body below her head. Underneath her chin, he becomes fascinated by the interplay between her tendrils of hair and the shadows they cast on her untanned flesh. Another woman called Ib (cat. 12) looks equally determined. She could be lying down, or simply propping her head against a wall. Either way, we can sense her inner determination and stoicism, as well as delighting once again in Freud's ability to define the discreet yet playful shadow left by her nose, lips and chin.

Reclining Figure 1994. Cat. 38-41

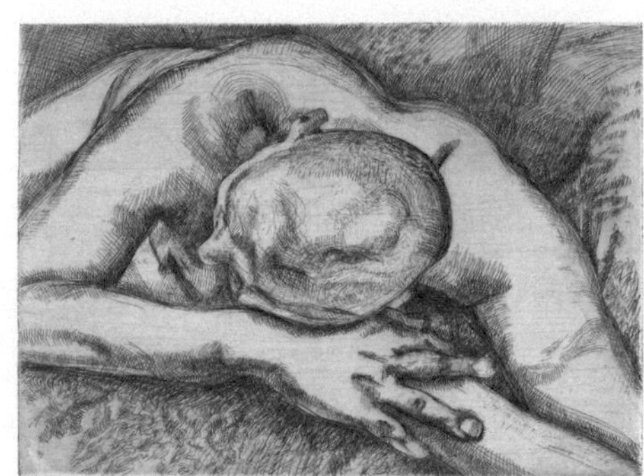

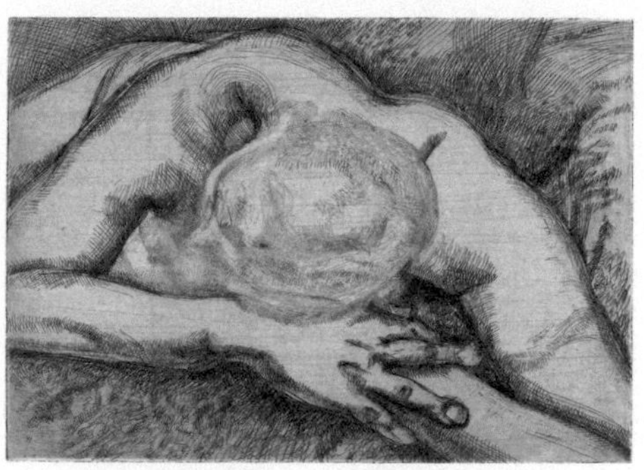

Every now and again, Freud produces an etching so sculptural in feeling that it helps to explain why he placed Rodin's bronze Balzac with such prominence in his house. The man called Kai (cat. 32) appears to have no intention of relaxing, let alone reclining on the artist's bed. He remains defiantly upright, and Freud emphasises the sprightliness of the hair enlivening his scalp, the impressive size of his forehead, the prominent bulk of his nose, the fleshiness of his lips and the sheer monumentality of a neck almost entirely swathed in dark shadow.

Nor does Freud find the spirit of well-constructed endurance in men alone. *Portrait Head* (cat. 62), the most recent etching in this collection, celebrates a similar sense of resilience. Sadness can be detected in her facial expression, especially around the eyebrows, suggesting that she has experienced difficulties during her life so far. All the same, Freud sees her fundamentally as a potent individual. The scarf around her neck suggests that she is feeling the winter cold. Unlike Kai, though, she looks up. Her mouth

conveys the hint of a smile as she stares forwards, insisting on visual observation as a prime means of comprehending the enigma of existence. Long hair flows down on to her shoulders and mingles with the scarf, thereby reinforcing the substance of her presence. Freud ensures that nothing in the background distracts us from this woman. The space around remains empty, allowing her to rise up like a mountain and assert a rugged endurance.

Elsewhere, two etchings in the collection show people who are virtually asleep: *Man Resting* (cat. 24) and *Woman with an Arm Tattoo* (cat. 53). But these are not simply images of relaxation. The model in *Man Resting* has a forehead creased with frowns, suggesting that he may at any instant open both his eyes and rediscover his tense engagement with the world. In *Woman with an Arm Tattoo*, Freud's sitter still seems vulnerable. Dark shadows can be detected beneath her eyes, and she parts her lips slightly as if impelled by an unconscious urge to speak. She looks tense rather than rested, and the

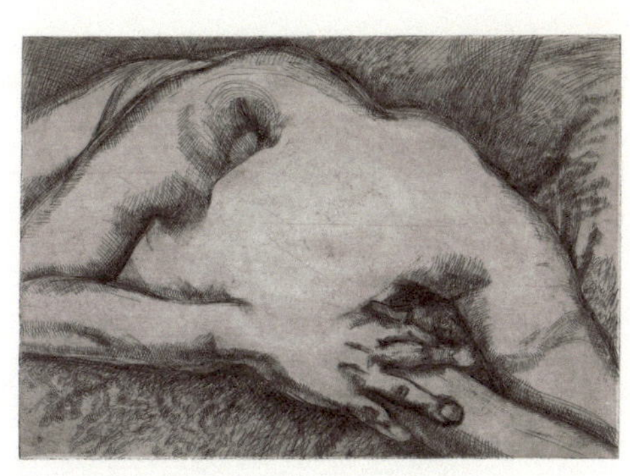

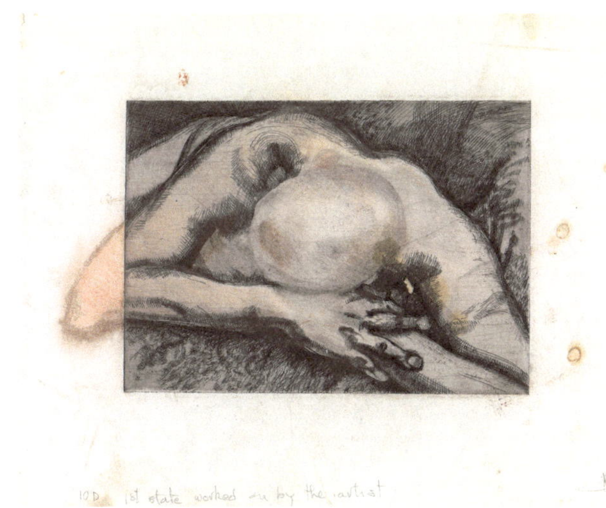

rather alarming pressure of her hand pushed against cheek, eye and nose adds to the feeling of oppression. Freud's ability to convey the texture of human flesh in all its tactile, living immediacy reinforces the sense of alarm. The woman may be asleep, yet she is far from torpid. Her mind seems to be caught up in a turbulent dream-world, just as Sigmund Freud might have expected.

Even when the model's eyes are open and staring straight out at us, as in *Head of a Naked Girl* (cat. 60), the decision to focus so tightly on the face makes us feel that we have been brought into contact with the model's thoughts. More, perhaps, than any other modern artist, Freud is able to expose the full psychological complexity of the people he studied with such probing intentness. When I asked him what were the works that really stood out for him from his long career, he answered after a long pause: "The ones I think are the most courageous and truth-telling. They come increasingly from early on. You have to know what the truth is before you

can tell it. I used to show off a lot, and I never believed in the idea of being a student. I didn't want the tentative thing that students have."

Several other etchings all emphasise wakeful-ness. Although Lord Goodman is wearing his yellow pyjamas, he looks obstinately alert (cat. 21). As Freud's lawyer for many years, he might well be listening to his client with exceptional care and diligence, weighing up in his own mind the questions he should ask Freud and the legal advice he must offer him. David Dawson (cat. 55), the only sitter who opens his mouth and bares his teeth, seems to be speaking. He leans for-ward and stares voraciously, as befits an artist who spends much of his time painting the observed world with avid attention. As for Freud's daughter Esther (cat. 30), who is a novel-ist, she stares into space with extraordinary power through enlarged eyes which appear fas-cinated by the sheer act of looking. She may well have inherited this intensity from her father, whose work is rooted in such a compulsive need to scrutinise and define.

Reclining Figure 1994. Cat. 42-45

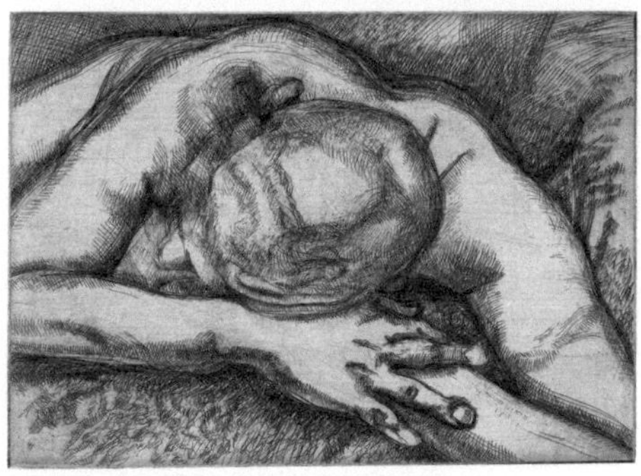

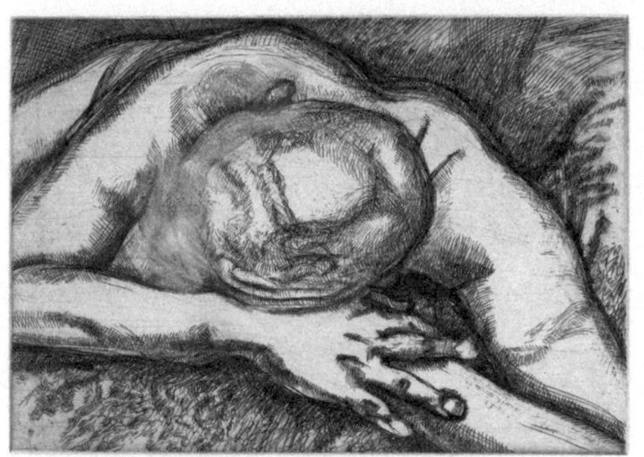

Sometimes, he turns his gaze on a mirror and studies himself alone. Using watercolour and graphite in his 1974 *Self-Portrait* (cat. 1), he becomes surprisingly free and indulges in impulsive swipes of colour which culminate in an electrifying passage of whiteness darting through his left ear. His head looks sun-tanned, and stands out against an unusually bleached background where his shirt disappears into a white void. But when Freud studies his features again, in an etching called *Self-Portrait: Reflection* (cat. 51) made twenty-two years later, he is surrounded by darkness. By this time he is 74 years old, and makes no attempt to minimise the effects of age on his gaunt, creased countenance.

Even so, his neck rises up from the base of the image with undaunted resolve. He has no intention of being defeated by the onset of old age, and stubbornly persists in affirming the pitted structure of his own head. The outcome has an authentic sense of grandeur, like a rock formation thrusting out of the earth and asserting its craggy presence in an otherwise empty, nocturnal landscape. This is a portrait of the artist as defiant survivor, an indomitable force who will never stop exploring, charting and interpreting the visible world for as long as his faculties allow.

With typical determination, Freud continued to work until illness finally forced him to stop. He died in July 2011 at the age of 88, leaving behind in the studio two etchings, a painting of a female nude and a portrait of his devoted assistant David Dawson, sitting naked beside the artist's whippet Eli. Freud was utterly uncompromising in his commitment to art. When visiting him, I was astonished to discover that he defied advancing years by devoting as many hours as possible to painting and print-making. Freud told me that he needed very little sleep, and would often work at night with even more energy than he had possessed during the day.

Around a decade before his death, he told me that his singleminded preoccupation with making art meant that he hardly ever left his studio: "I never see anyone, or go anywhere." He was

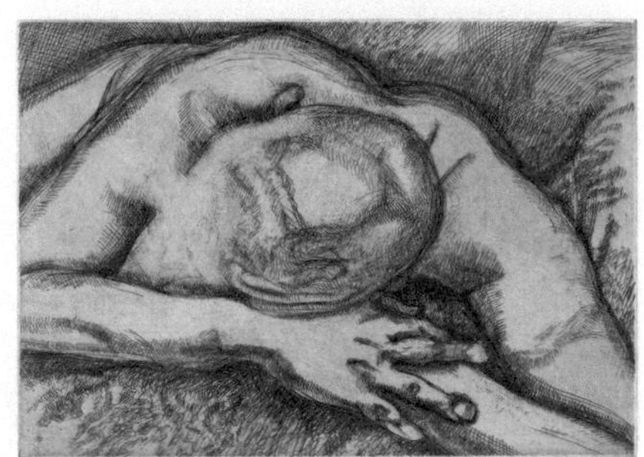

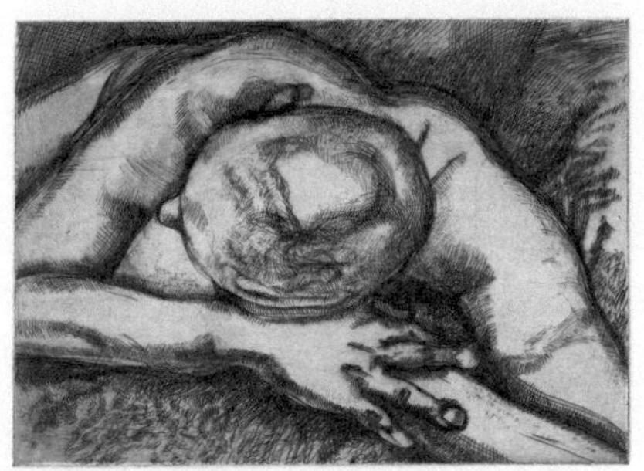

also increasingly determined to conserve all his energies for work. "I know I don't have much time left", he admitted. "I'm full of aches and pains, and I wake up in the middle of the night when I should be sleeping. So I want to paint as much as possible. I'd like, ideally, to die with brush in hand in the studio."

Hence the remarkable intensity of the images he managed to produce. Working steadily, and continuing to insist on an extraordinary number of sessions from the people who agreed to pose for him, he succeeded in exploring the reality of human life with far greater profundity than most figurative painters. While remaining fascinated by flesh, especially when it begins to burgeon, wither and crinkle with age, Freud also wanted to define the essential underlying spirit of the many different individuals he scrutinised. That is why we feel, when looking at his finest work, that he probed far below the surface and arrived at their essential selves.

Richard Cork (b. 1947) is a critic and curator. Cork has written about art, broadcasted on the BBC, curated exhibitions at Tate, Hayward Gallery, Royal Academy and Barbican Art Gallery, and published award-winning books and four volumes of writings on modern art. His books include *Art Beyond the Gallery; David Bomberg; A Bitter Truth – Avant-Garde Art and the Great War; Jacob Epstein; Michael Craig-Martin; Wild Thing*; and *The Healing Presence of Art: A History of Western Art in Hospitals*.

Reclining Figure 1994. Cat. 46-47

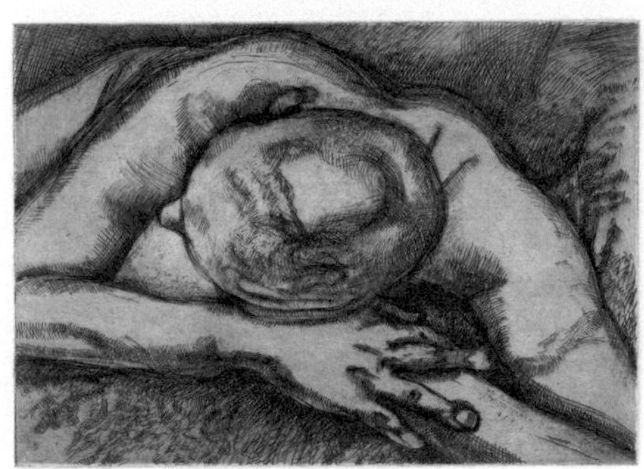

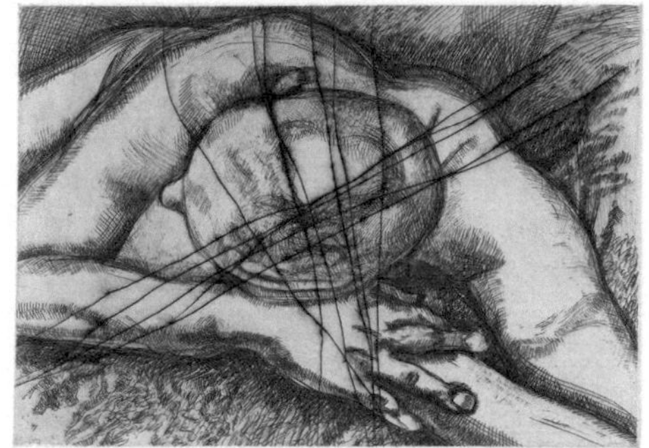

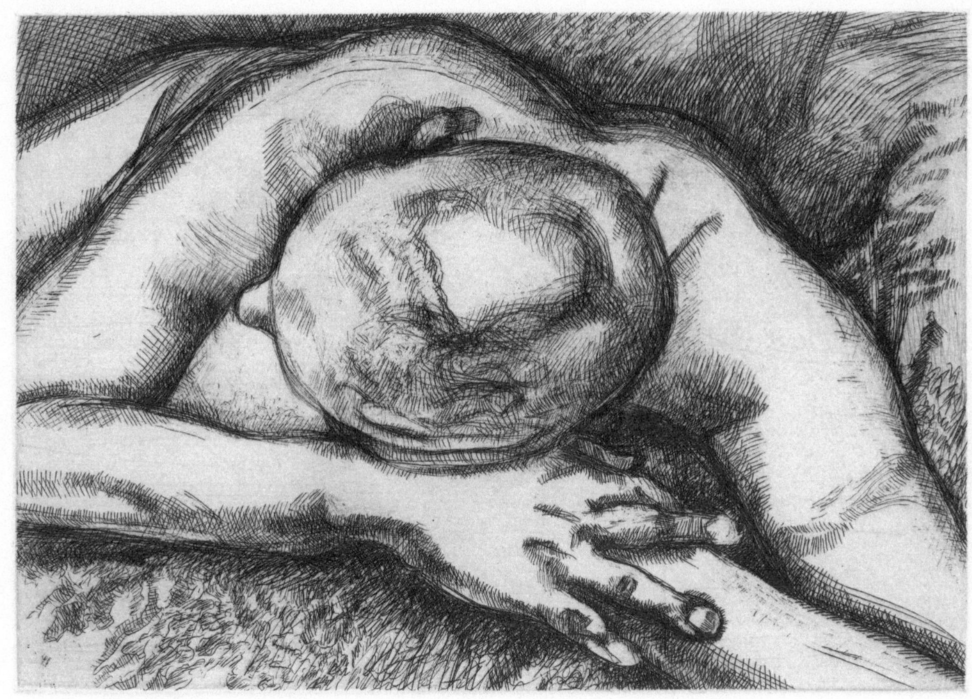

Reclining Figure. 1994. Cat. 48

Plates

   Self-Portrait. 1974. Cat. 1

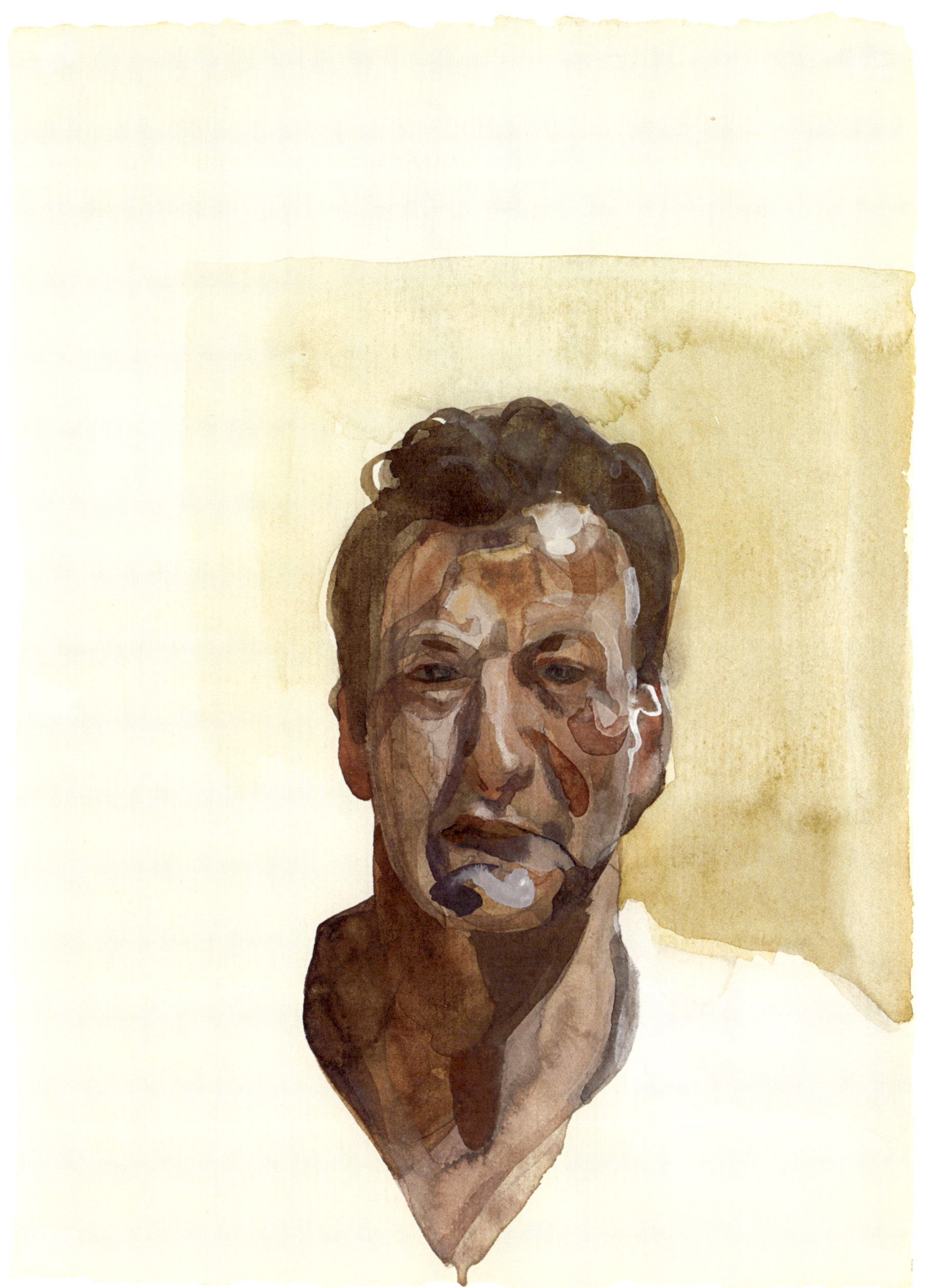

   Head and Shoulders. 1982. Cat. 4

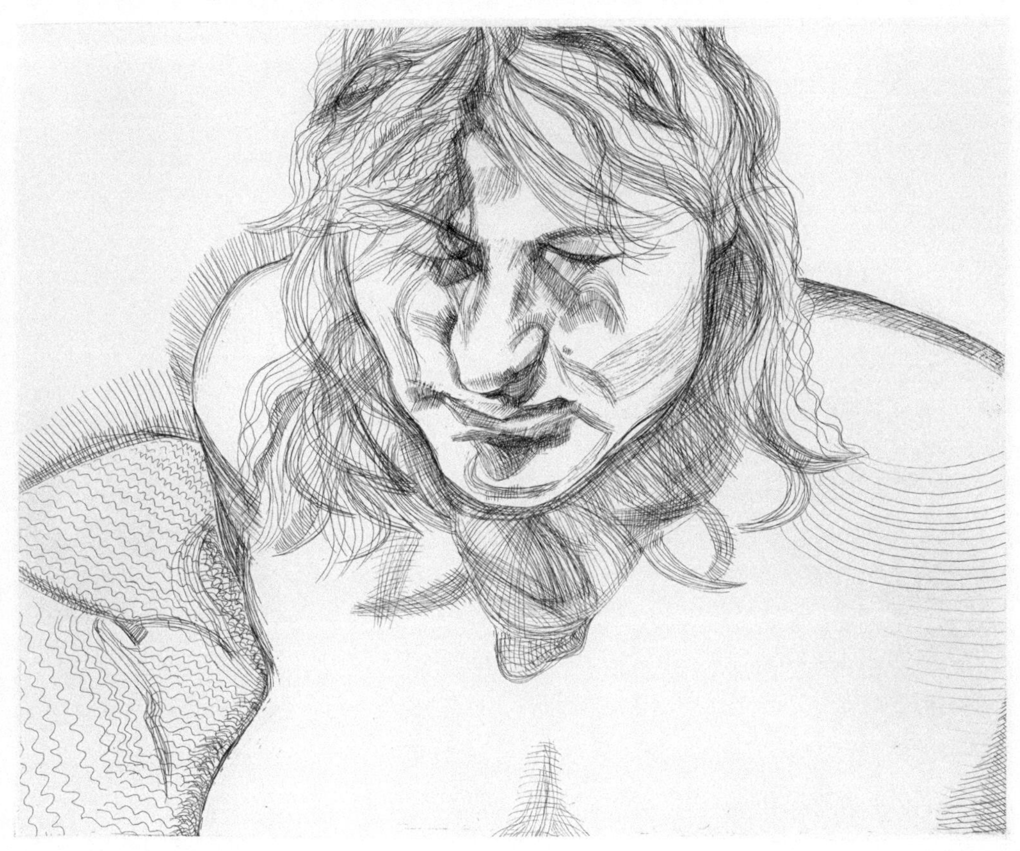

A/P IV/VIII   L.F.

    Bella. 1982. Cat. 3

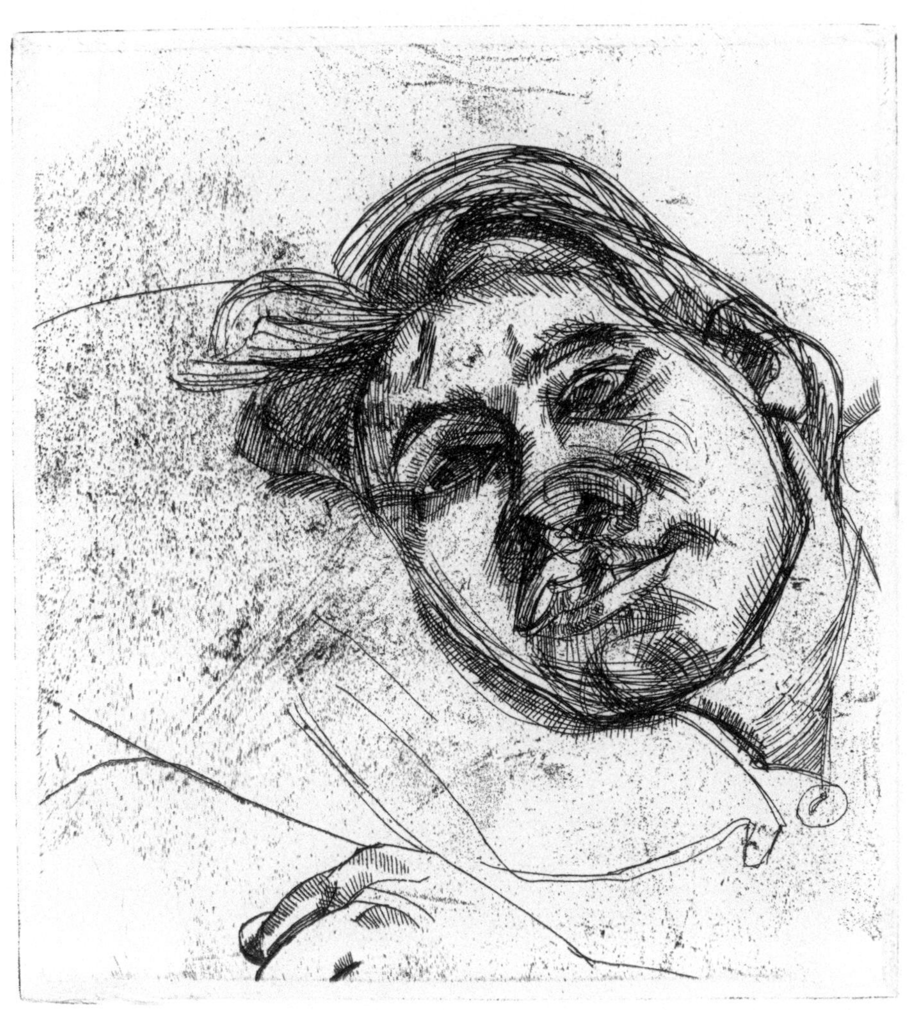
A/P II/X
L.F.

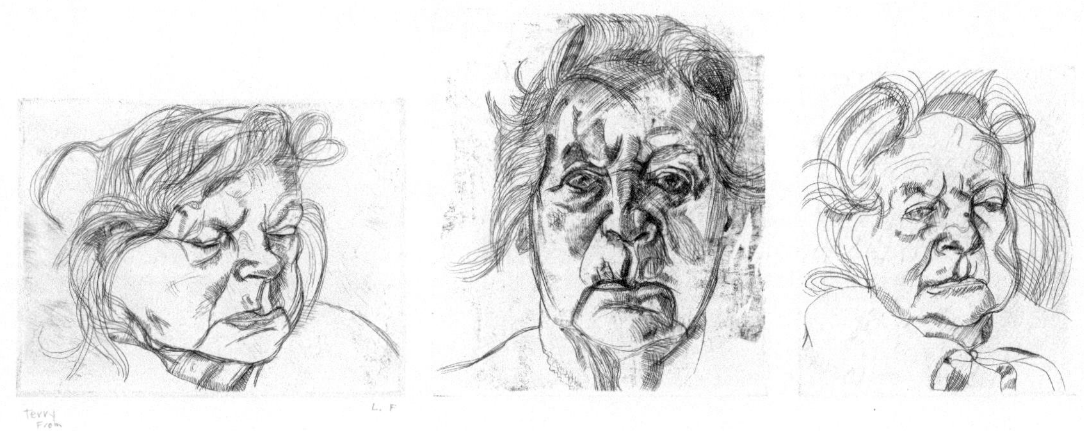
Terry
From
L. F

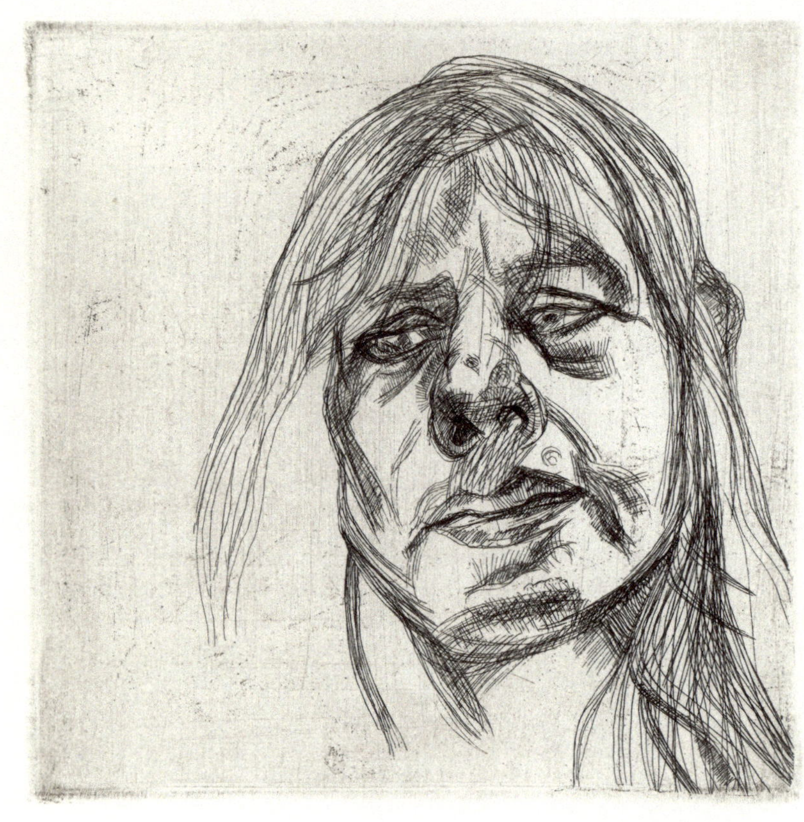

 Head of a Woman. 1982. Cat. 7 / *Head of Girl I*. 1982. Cat. 5

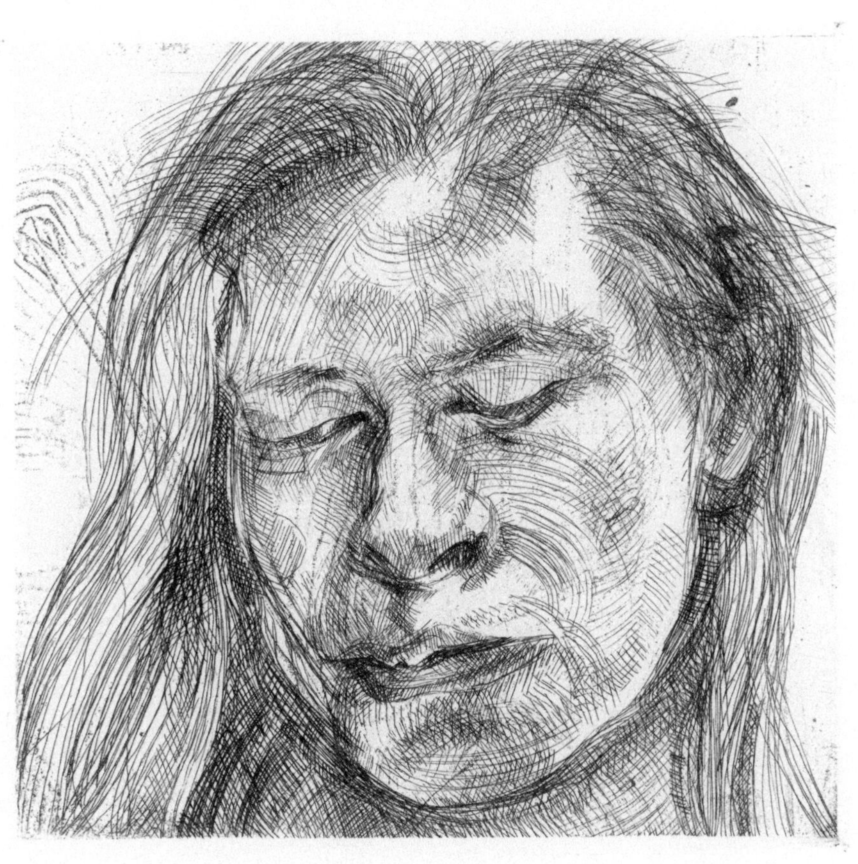
12/16
L. F

	Head of Girl II. 1982. Cat. 6

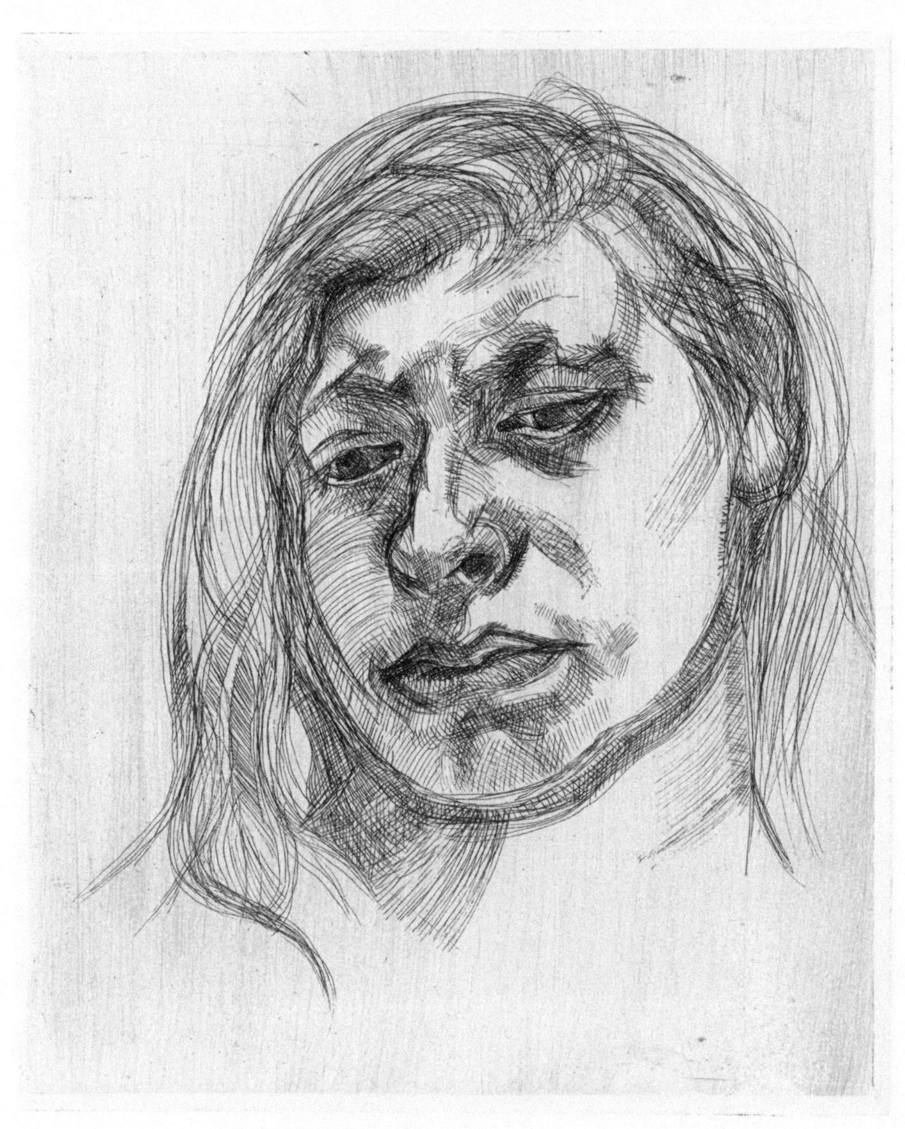

proof

L.F.

   A Couple. 1982. Cat. 2

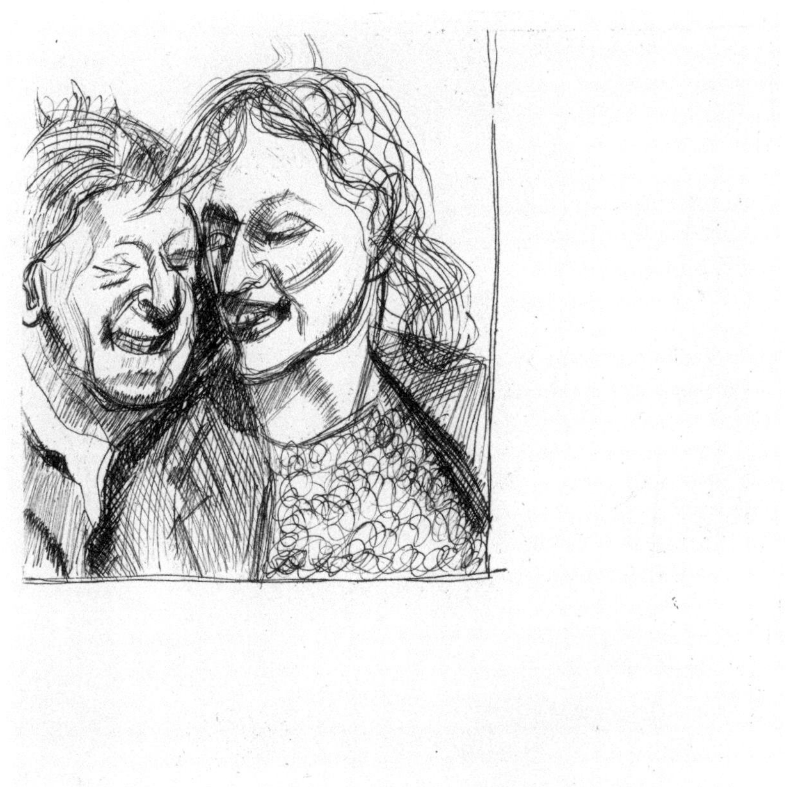

22/25   L. F.

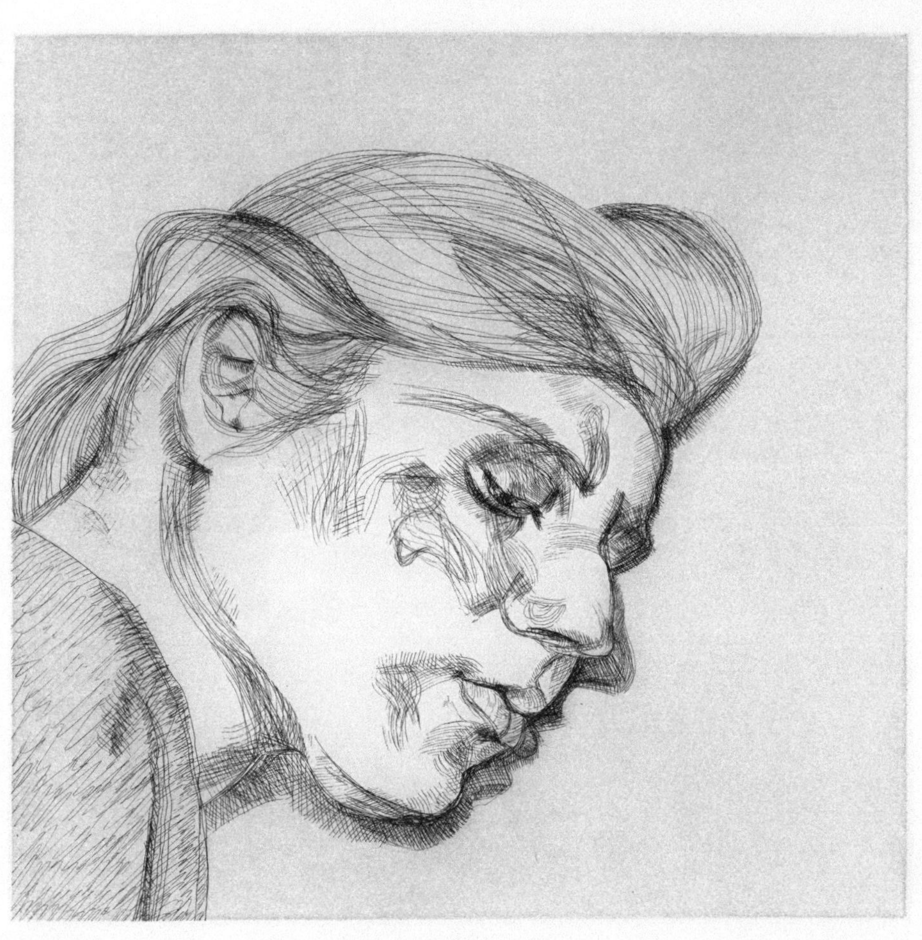

37/50
L.F.

 Head of Bruce Bernard. 1985. Cat. 15

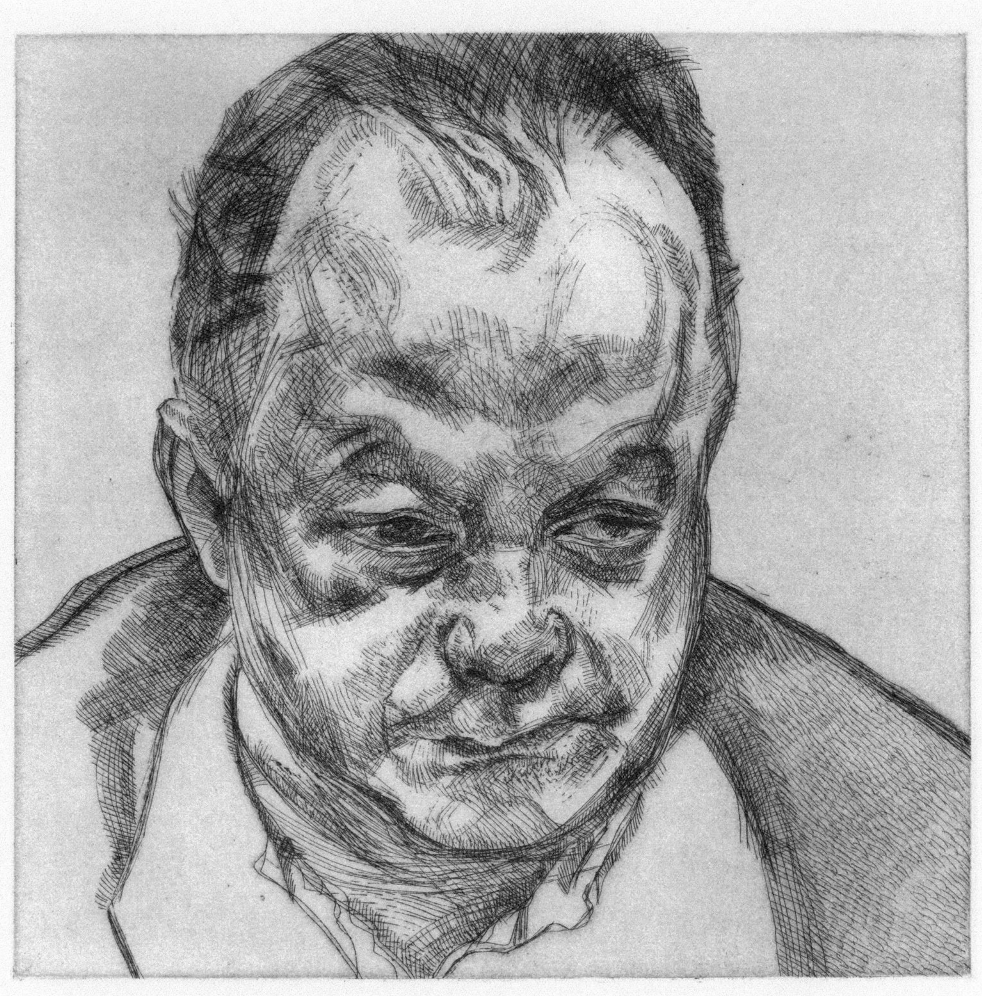

46/50

L. F

  Blond Girl. 1985. Cat. 13

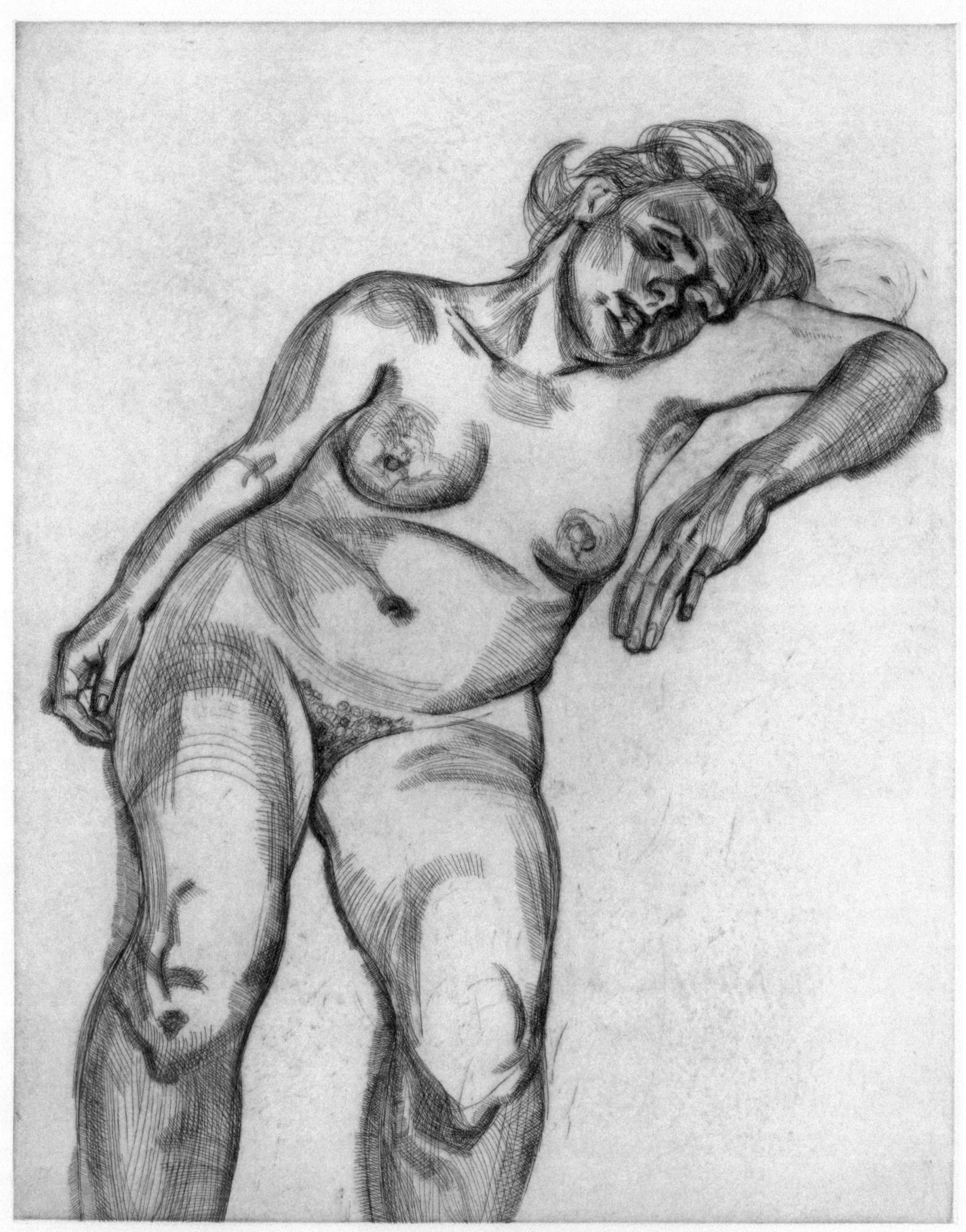

25/50

L.F

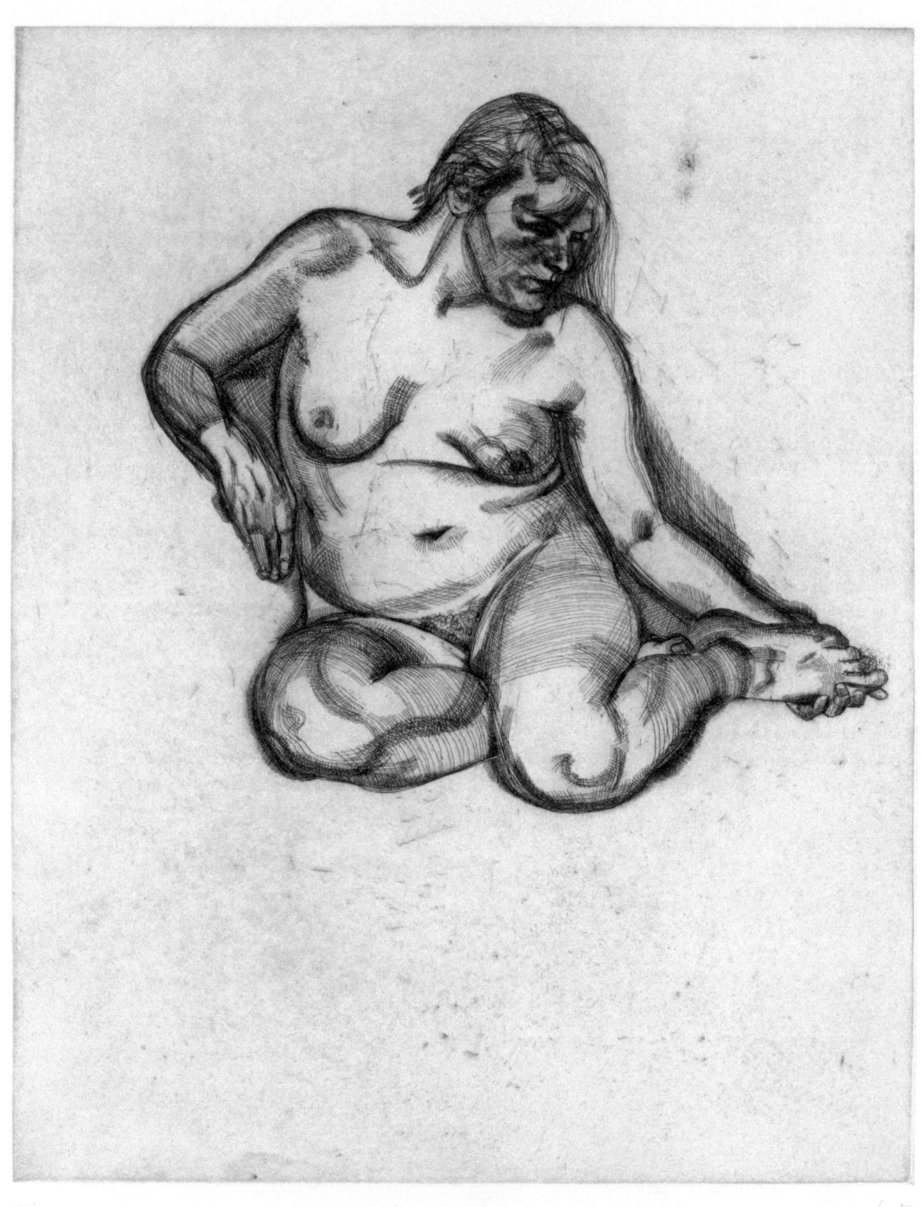

   Girl Holding Her Foot. 1985. Cat. 14 / *Man Posing.* 1985. Cat. 16

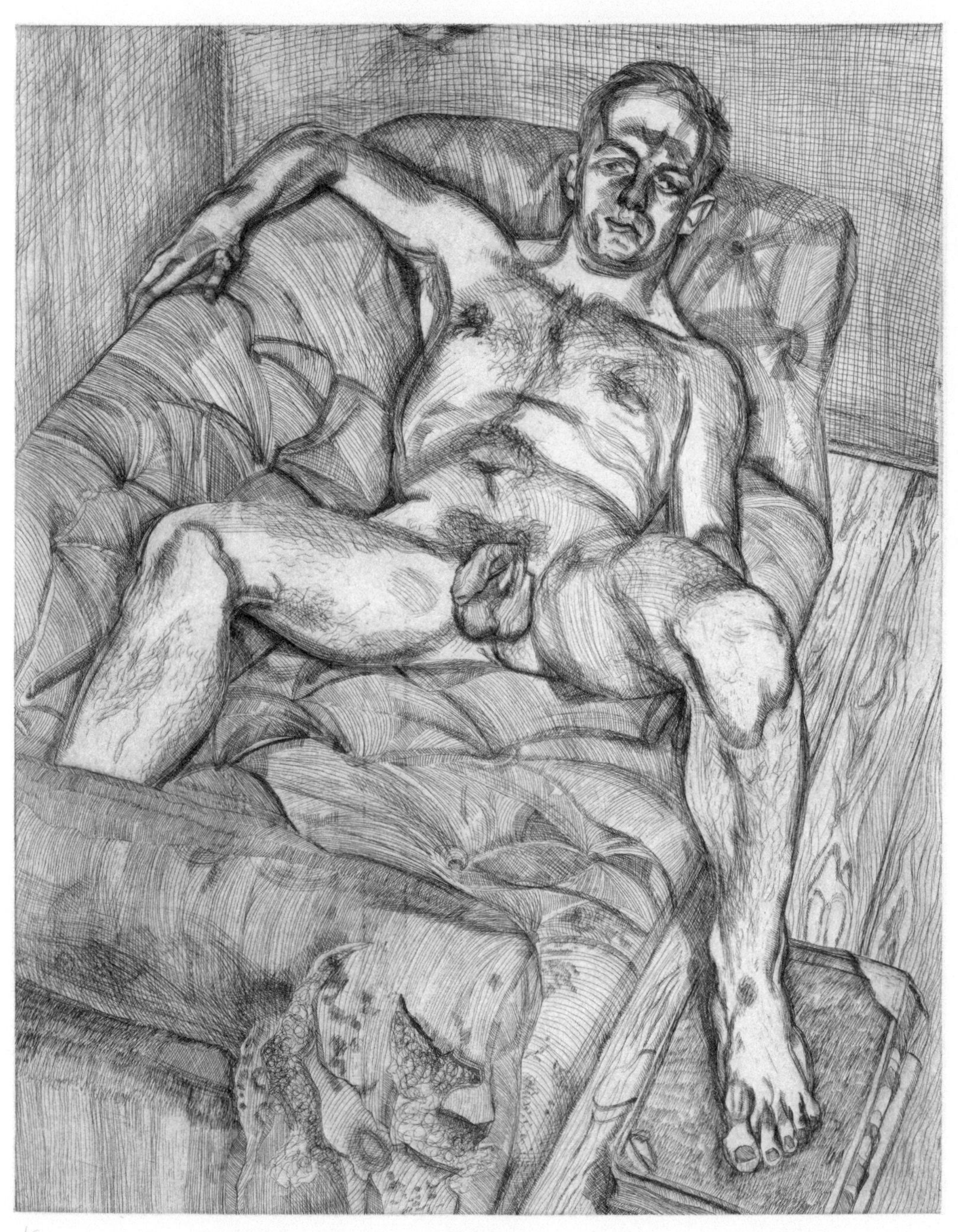

16/50

   Head of a Man. 1987. Cat. 20

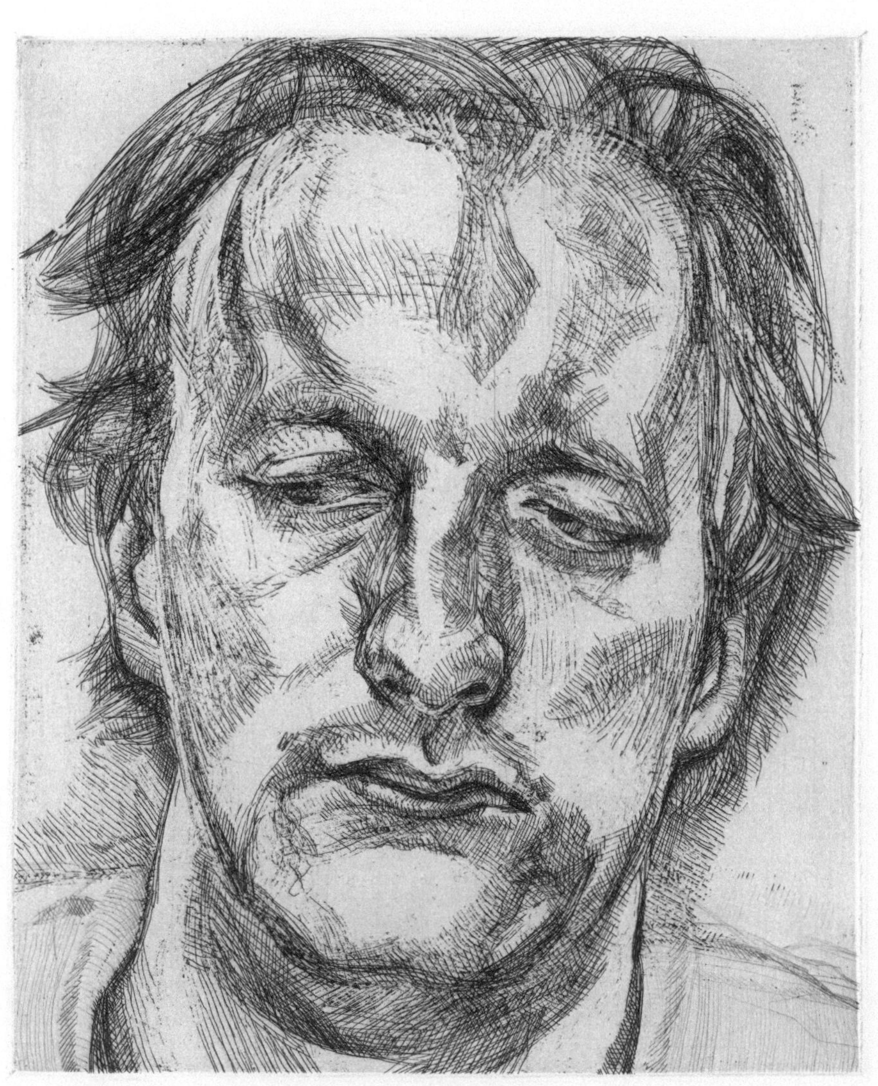
A. P
111/X
L.F.

    Naked Man on a Bed. 1987. Cat. 22

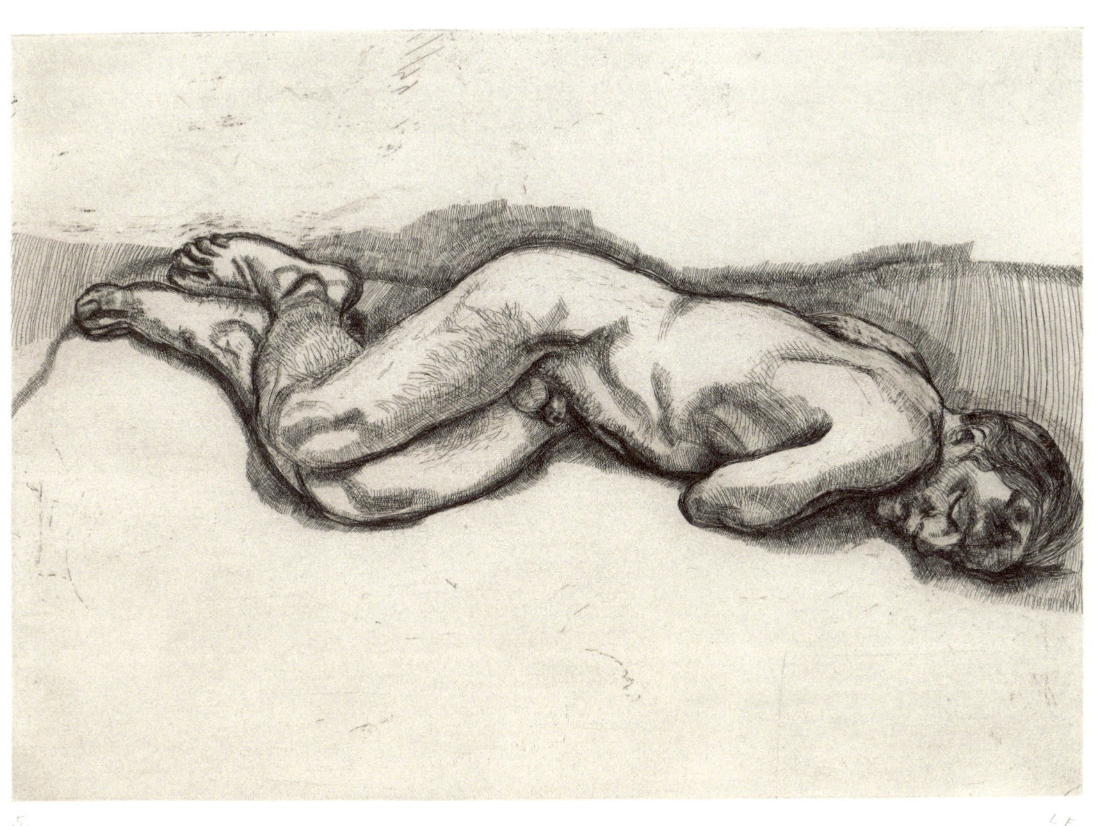

5/10

   Lord Goodman in His Yellow Pyjamas. 1987. Cat. 21

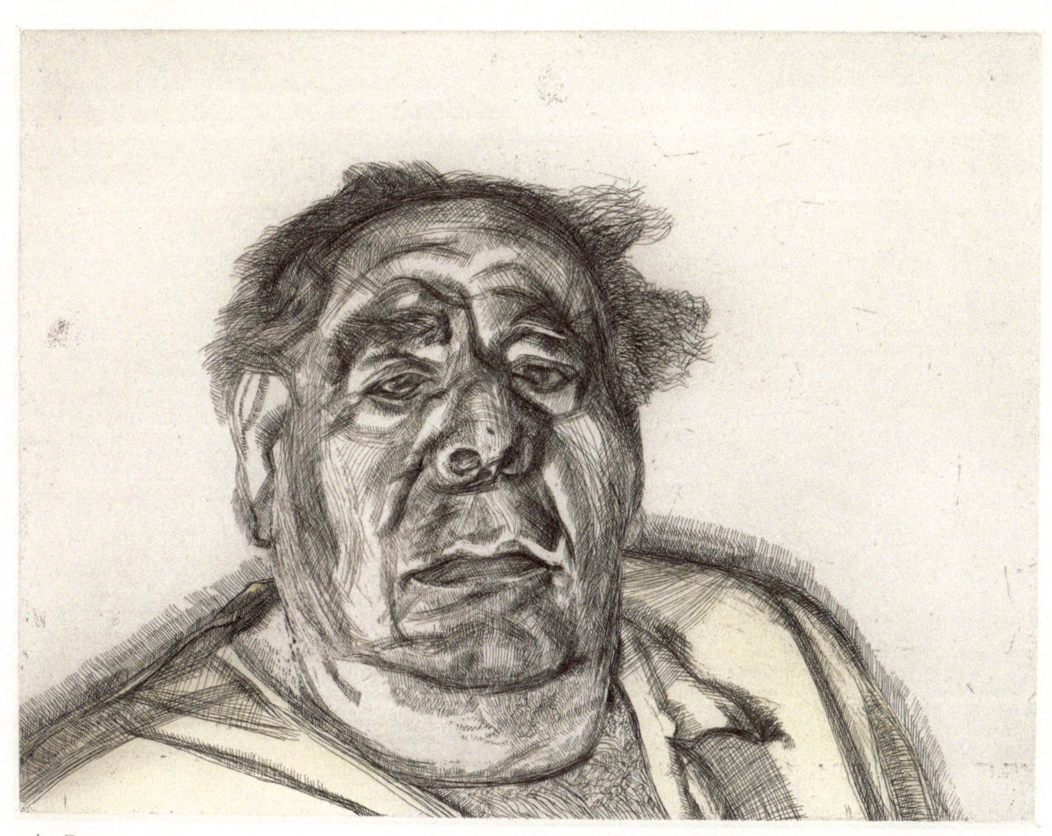

A.P. IV/X   L.F.

 Bella. 1987. Cat. 18

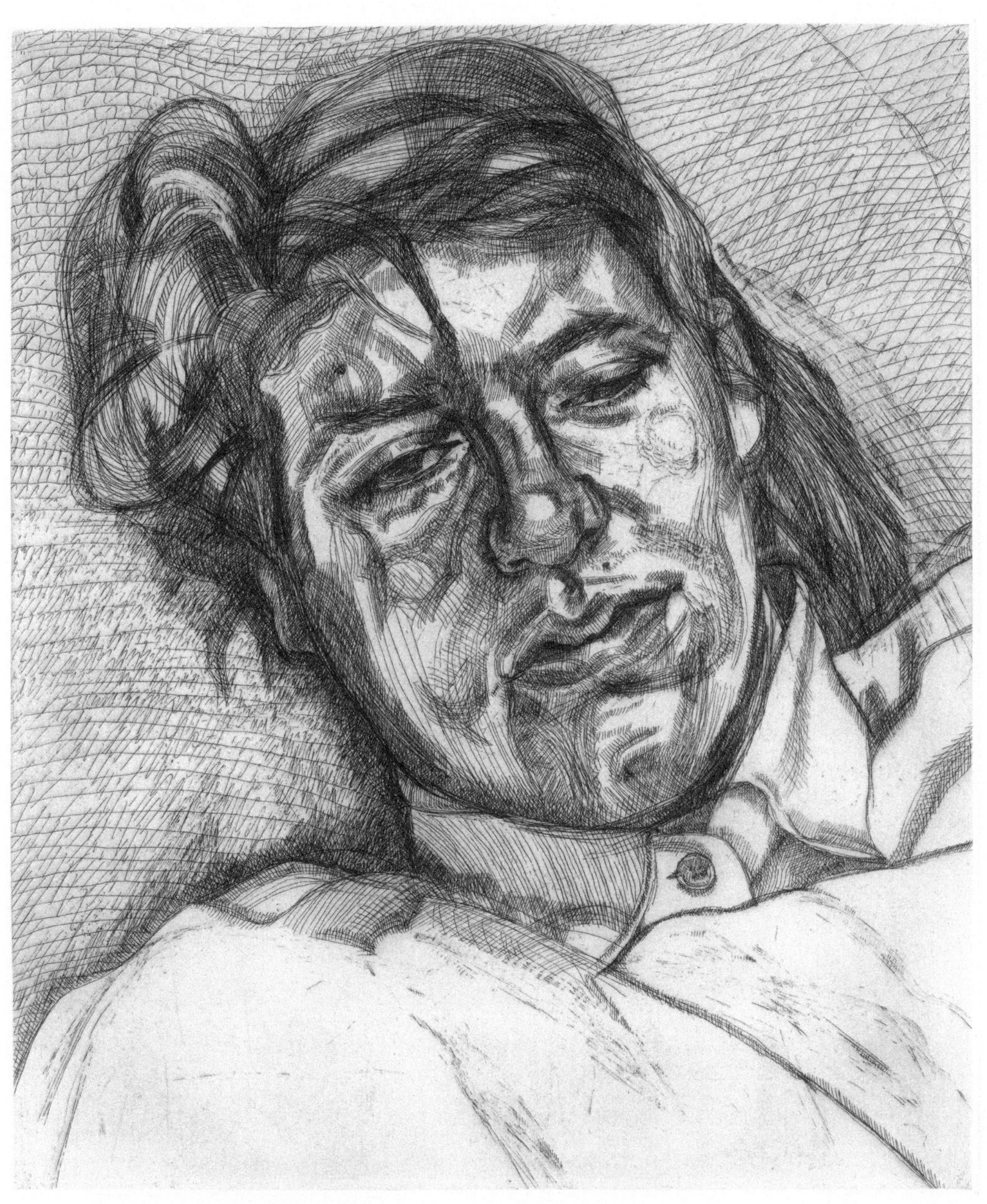

45/50   L.F

   Girl Sitting. 1987. Cat. 19

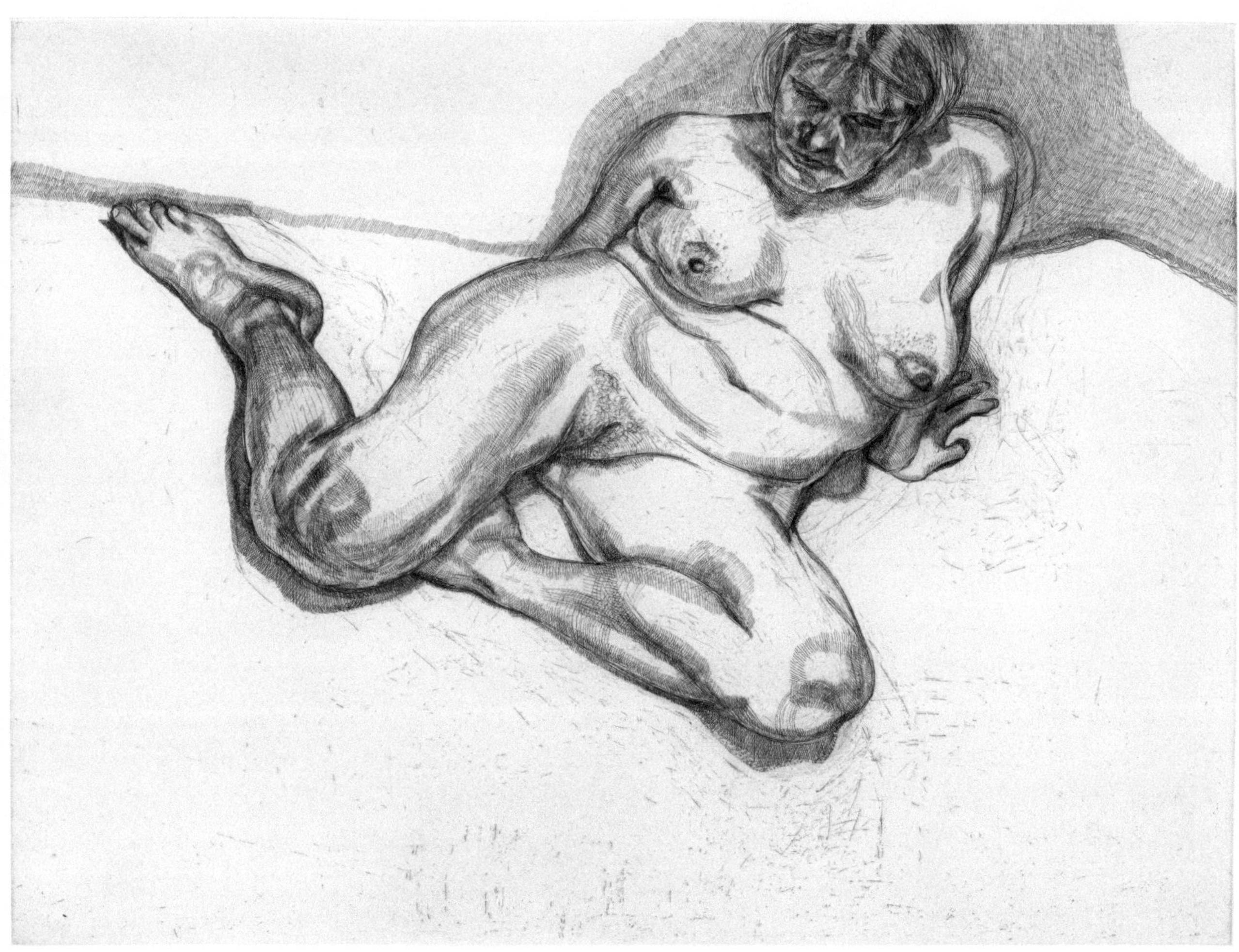

45/50   L.F.

   Man Resting. 1988. Cat. 24

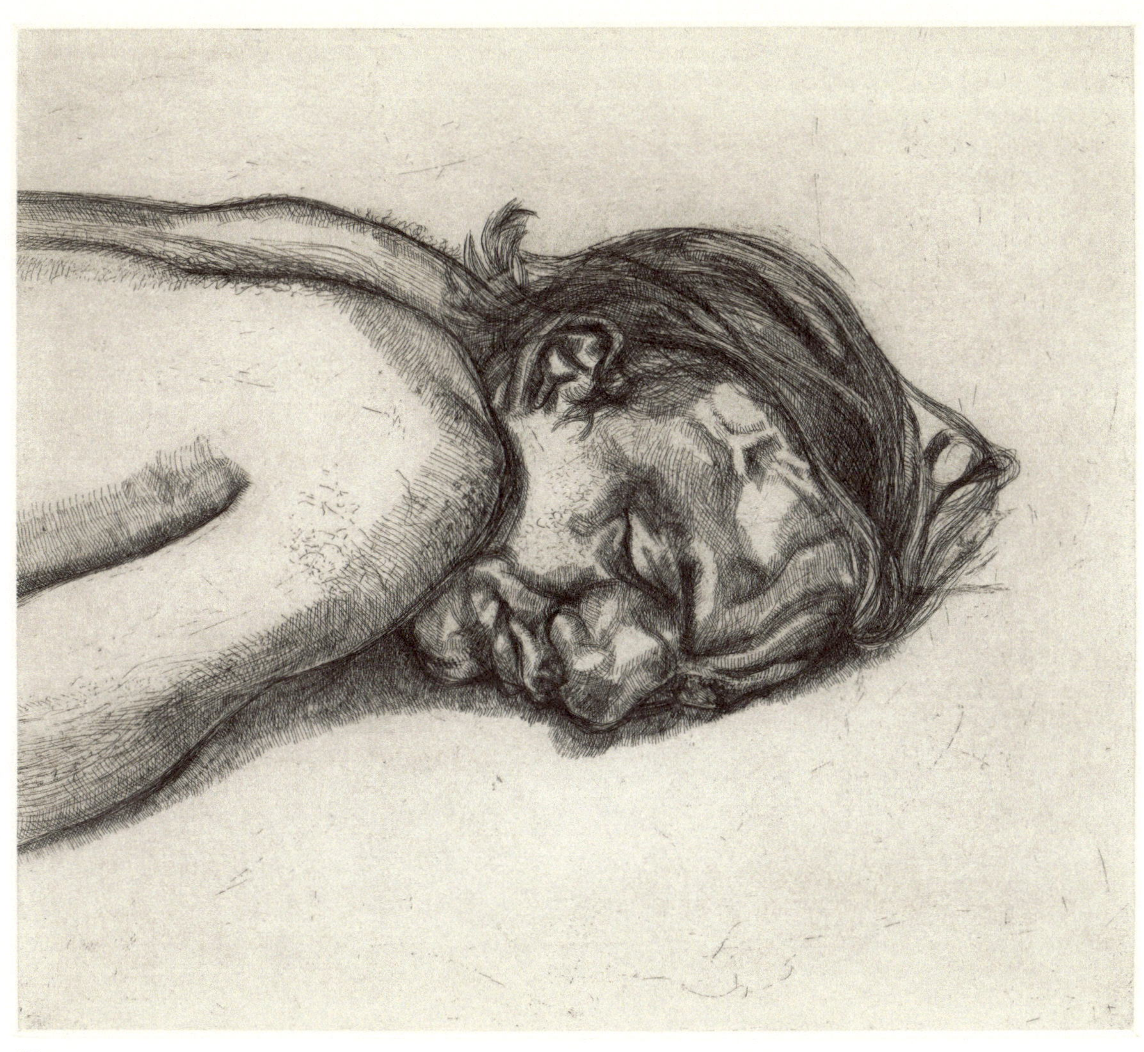

 Head of Ib. 1988. Cat. 23

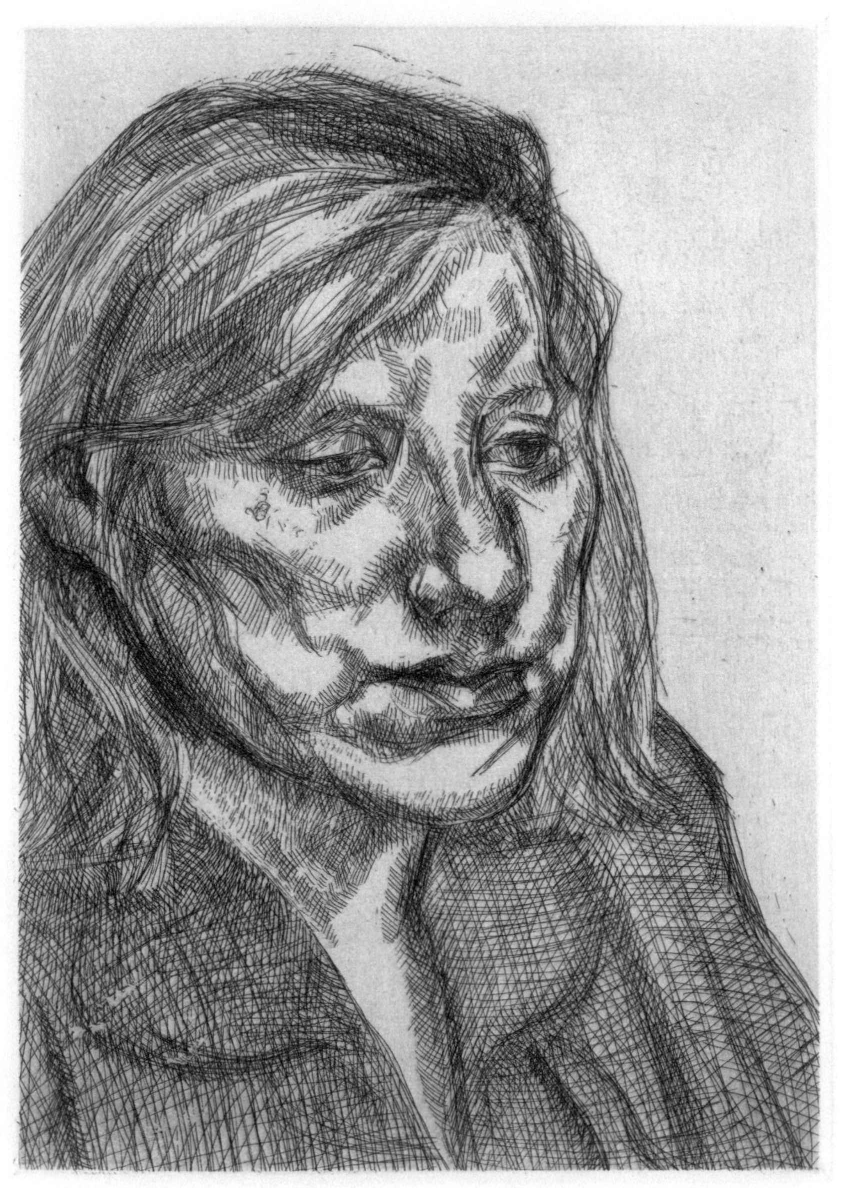

17/40   L F

   Cerith. 1989. Cat. 26

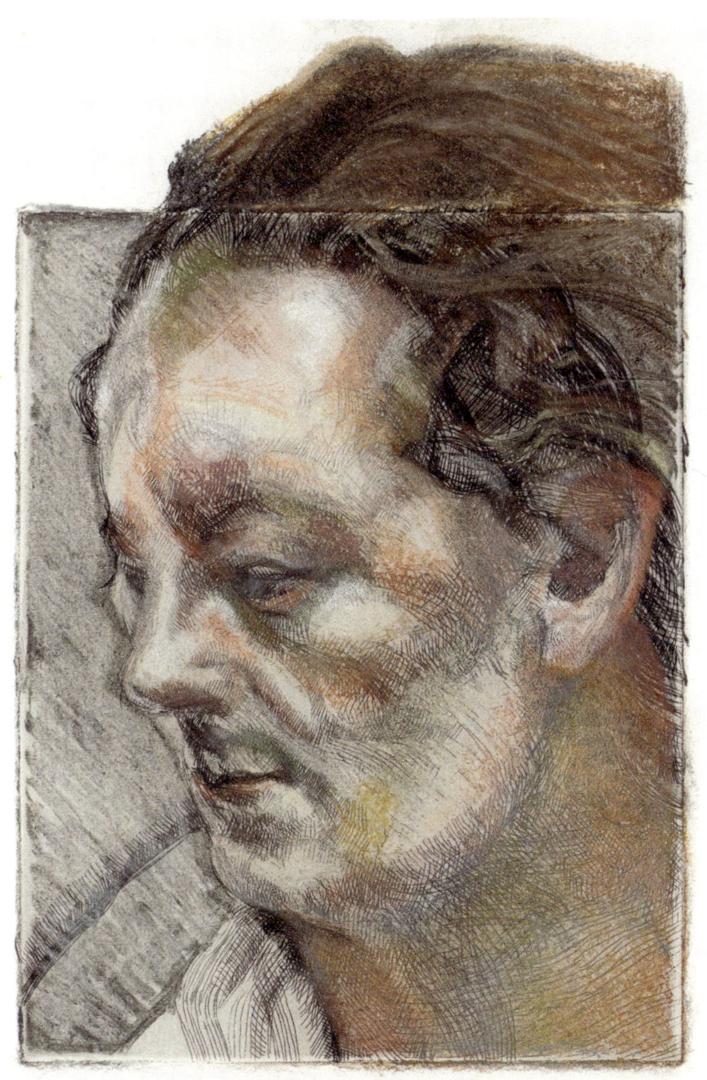

 Two Men in the Studio. 1989. Cat. 27

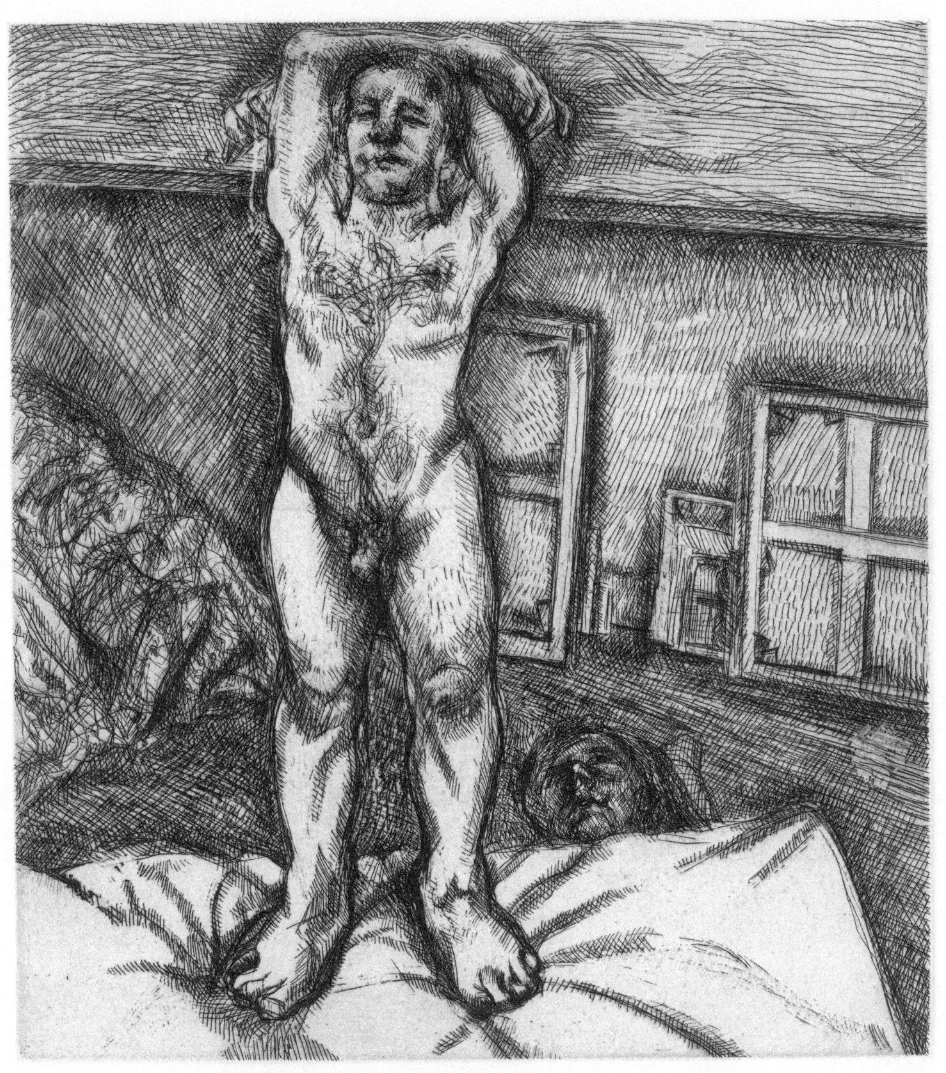

6/25
L.F

    Head and Shoulders of a Girl. 1990. Cat. 28

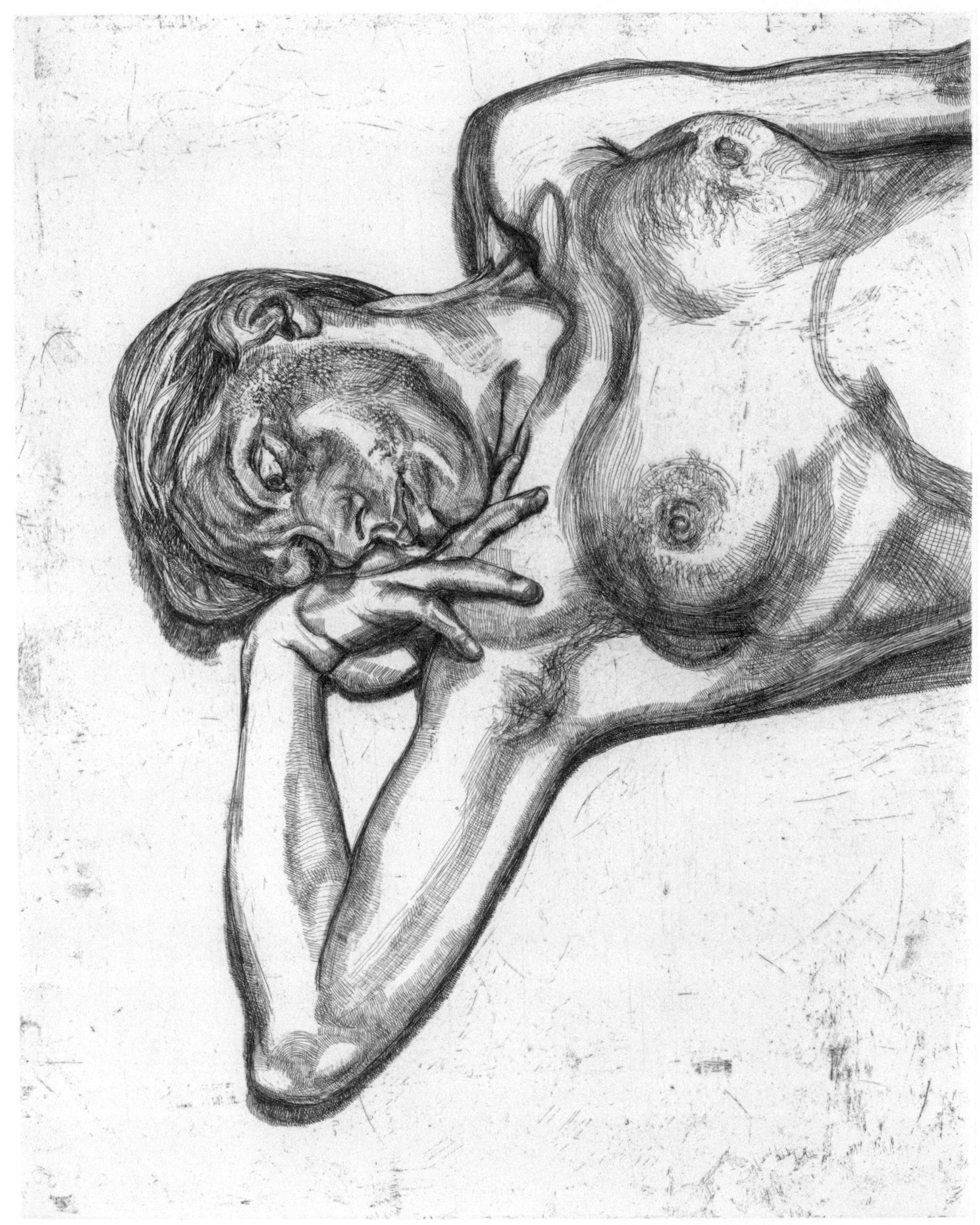

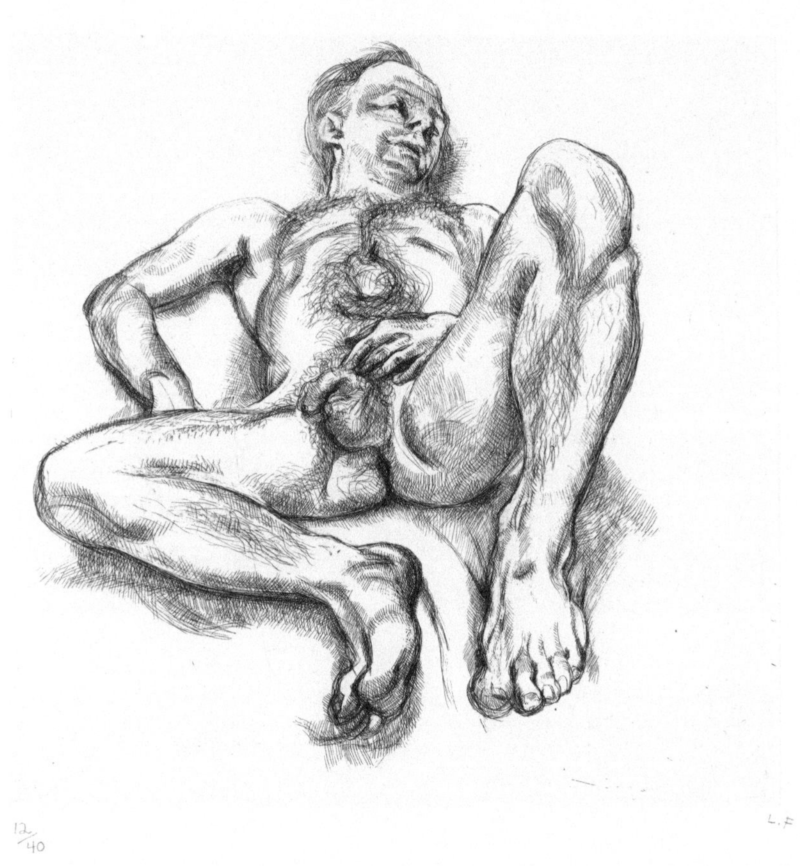

12/40
L.F

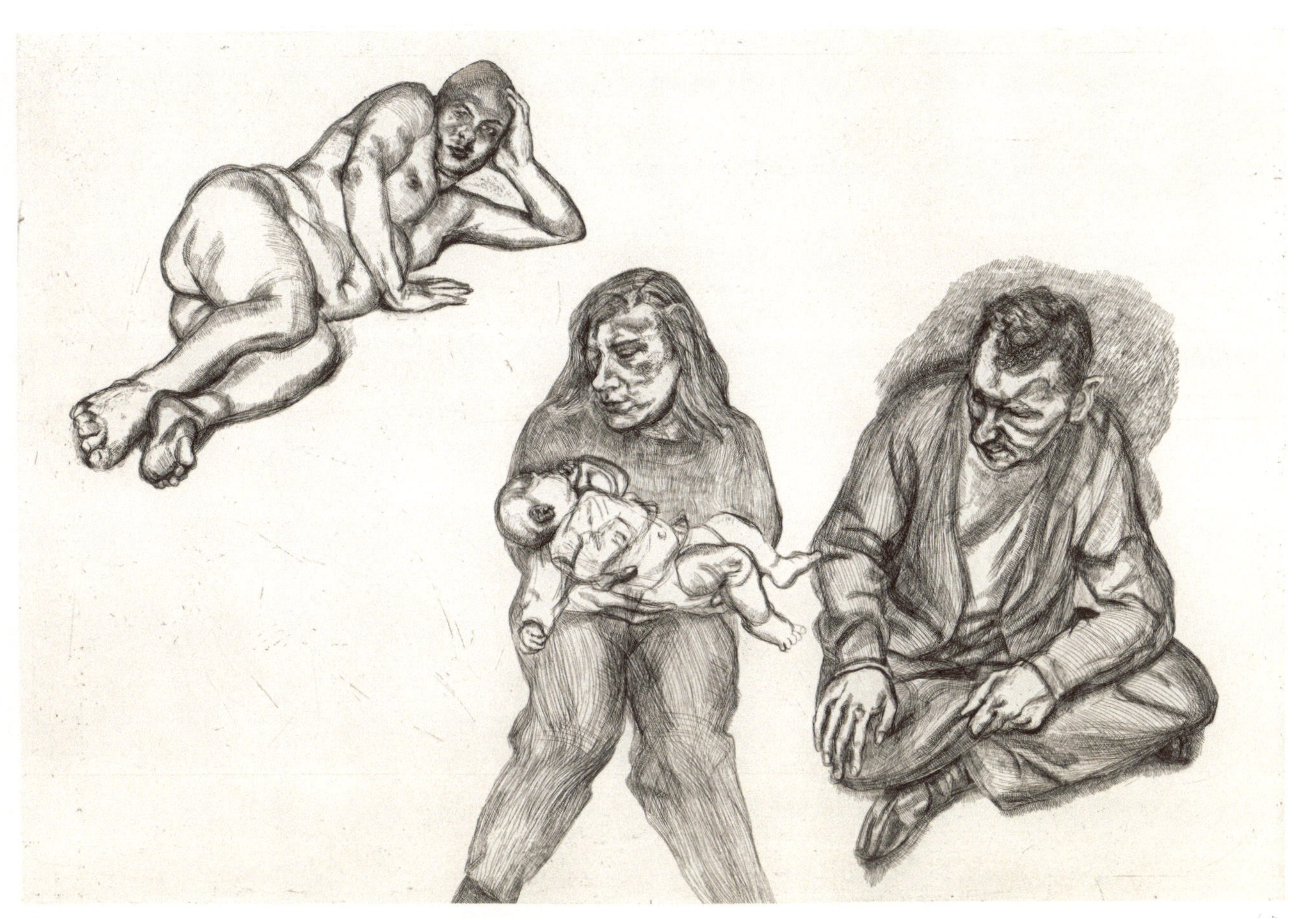

    Esther. 1991. Cat. 30

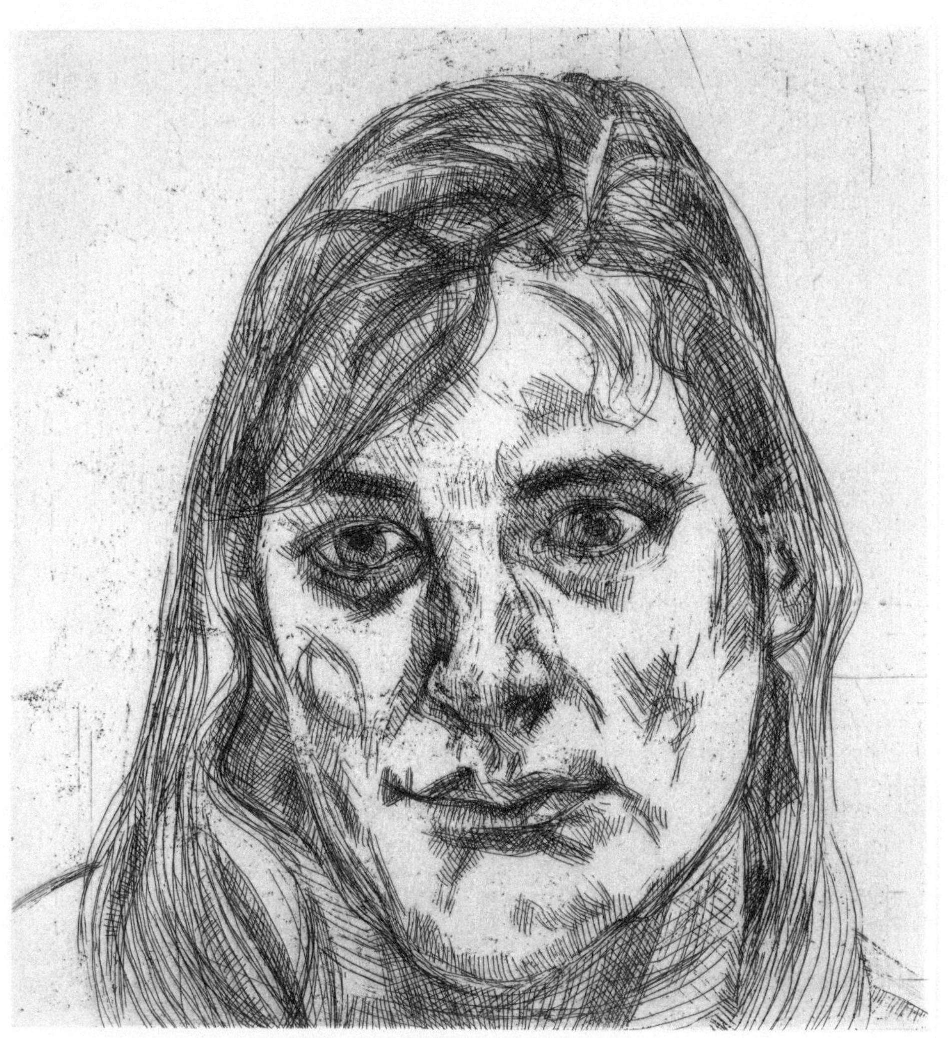

6/25
L.F

 Woman on a Bed. 1991-92. Cat. 33

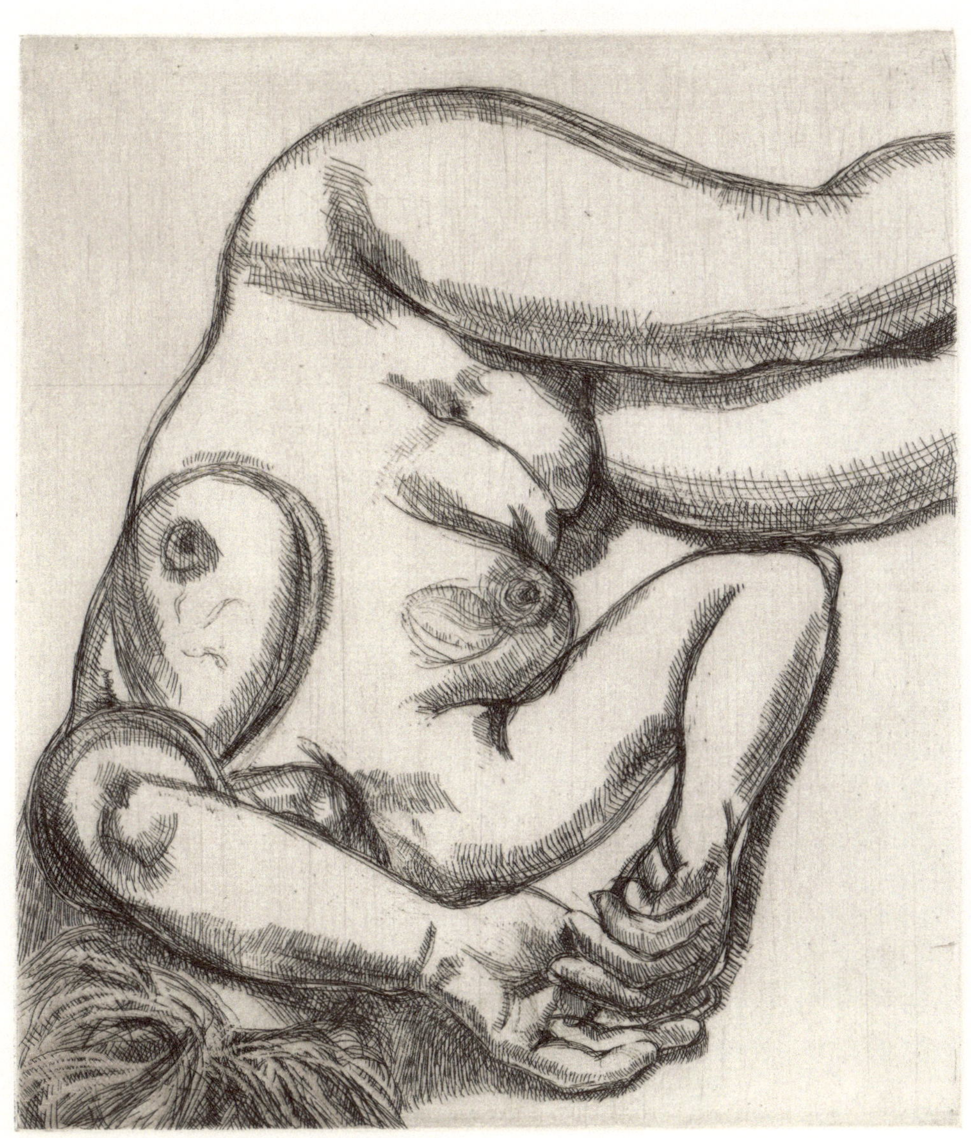

22/30

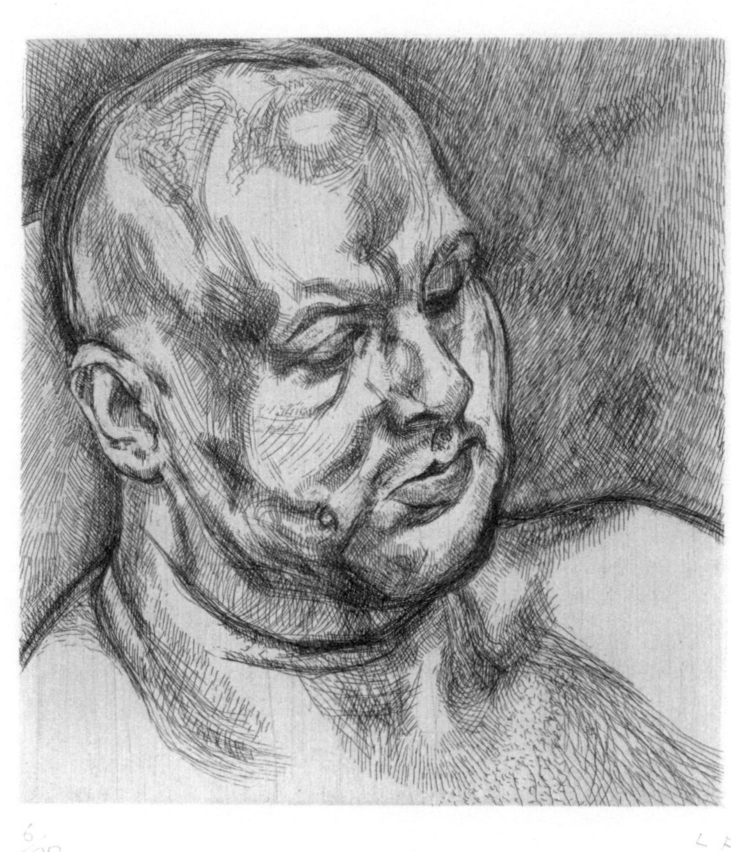

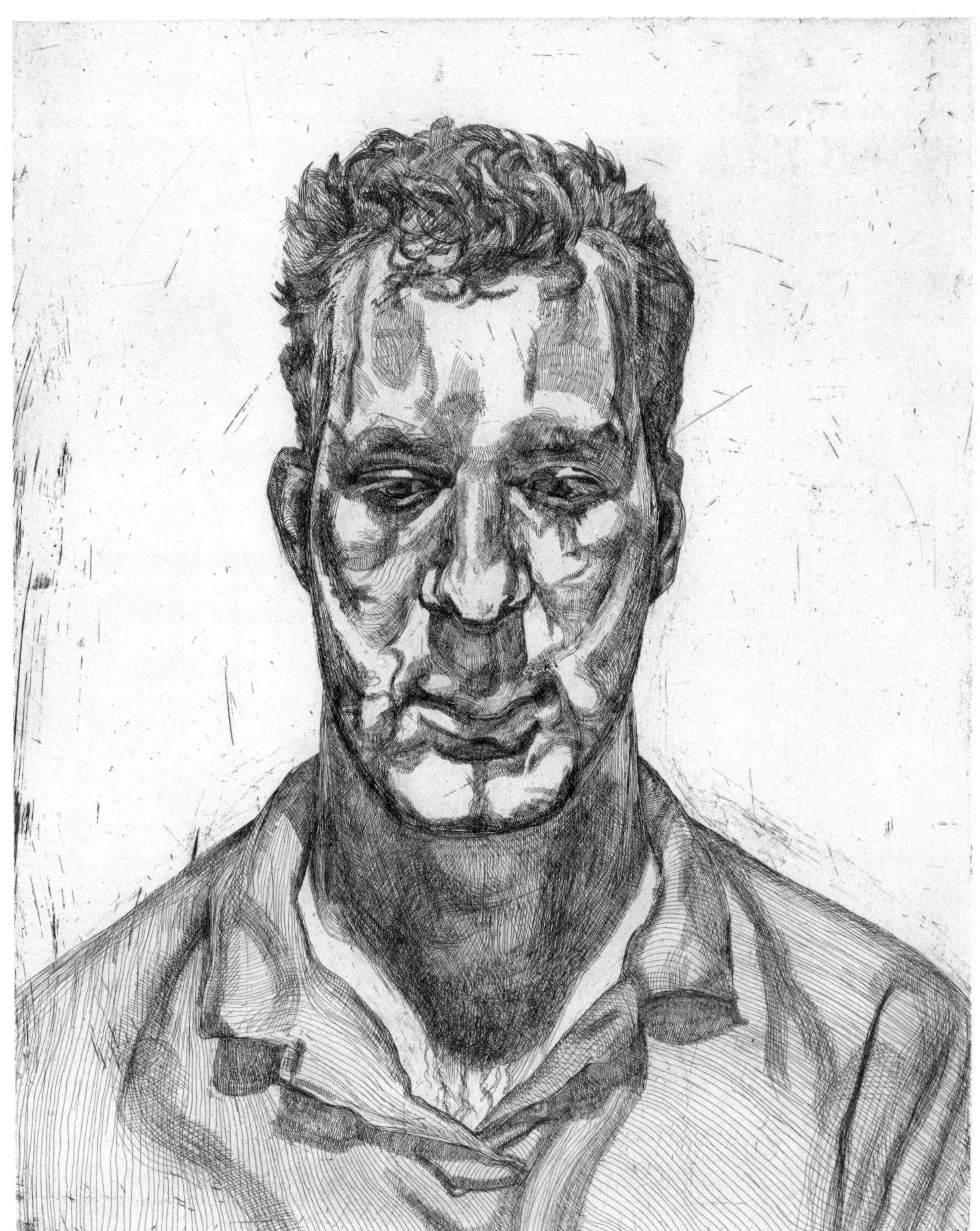

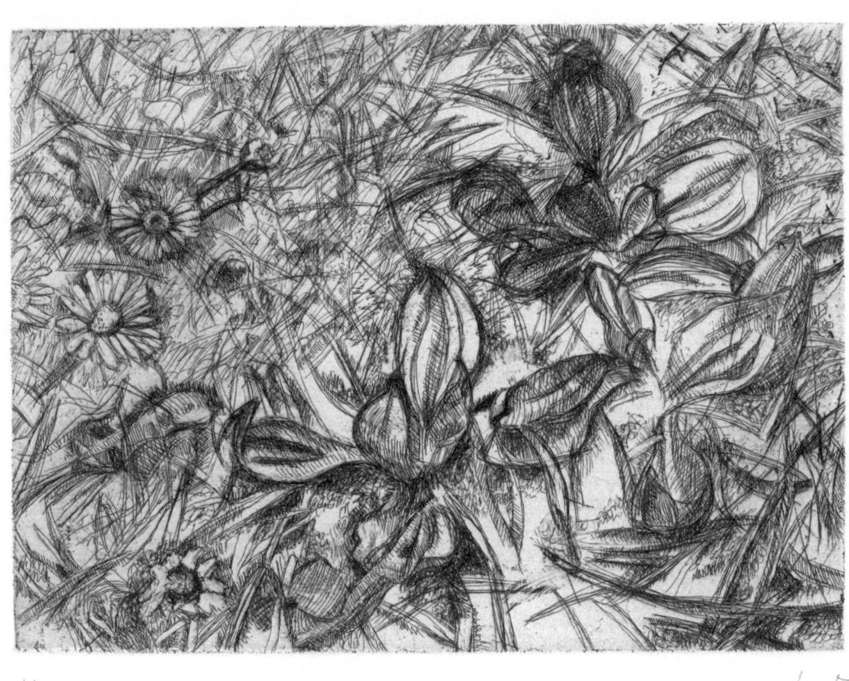

  Landscape. 1993. Cat. 35 / *Thistle.* 1985. Cat. 17

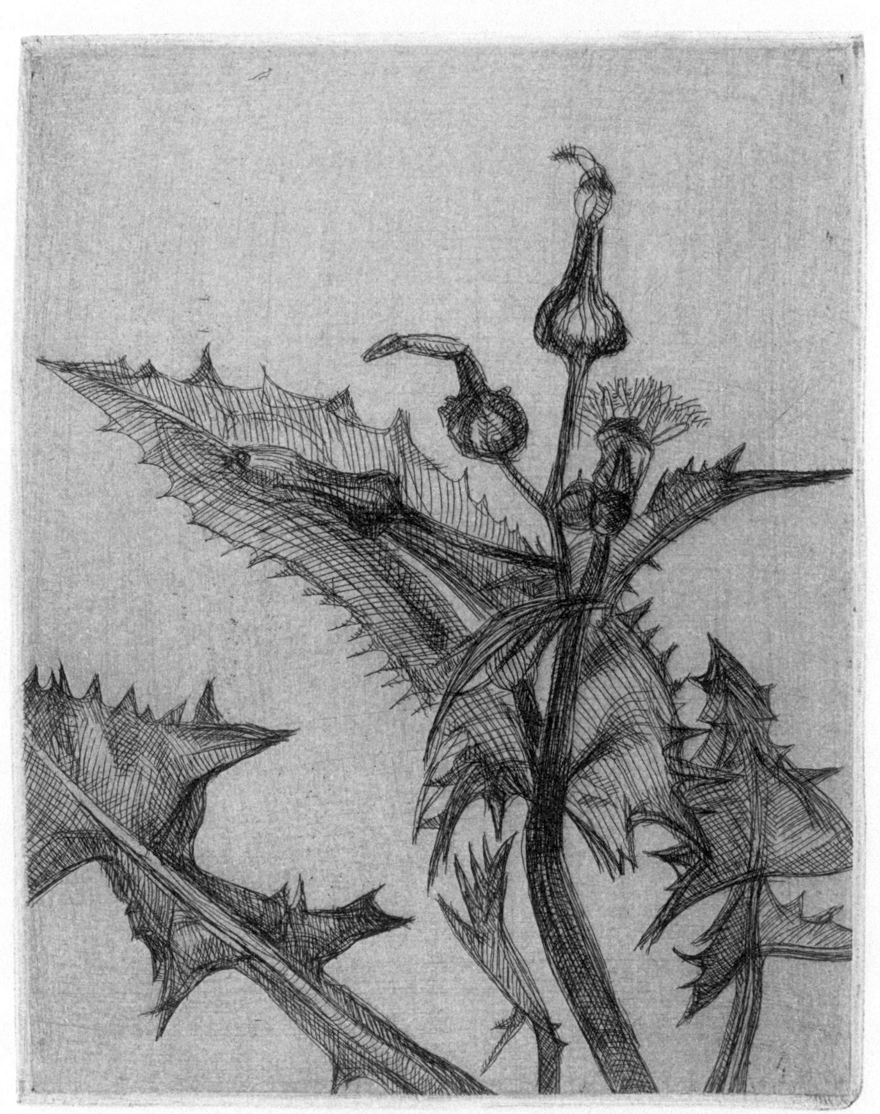

AP
V/VIII
LF

 Large Head. 1993. Cat. 36

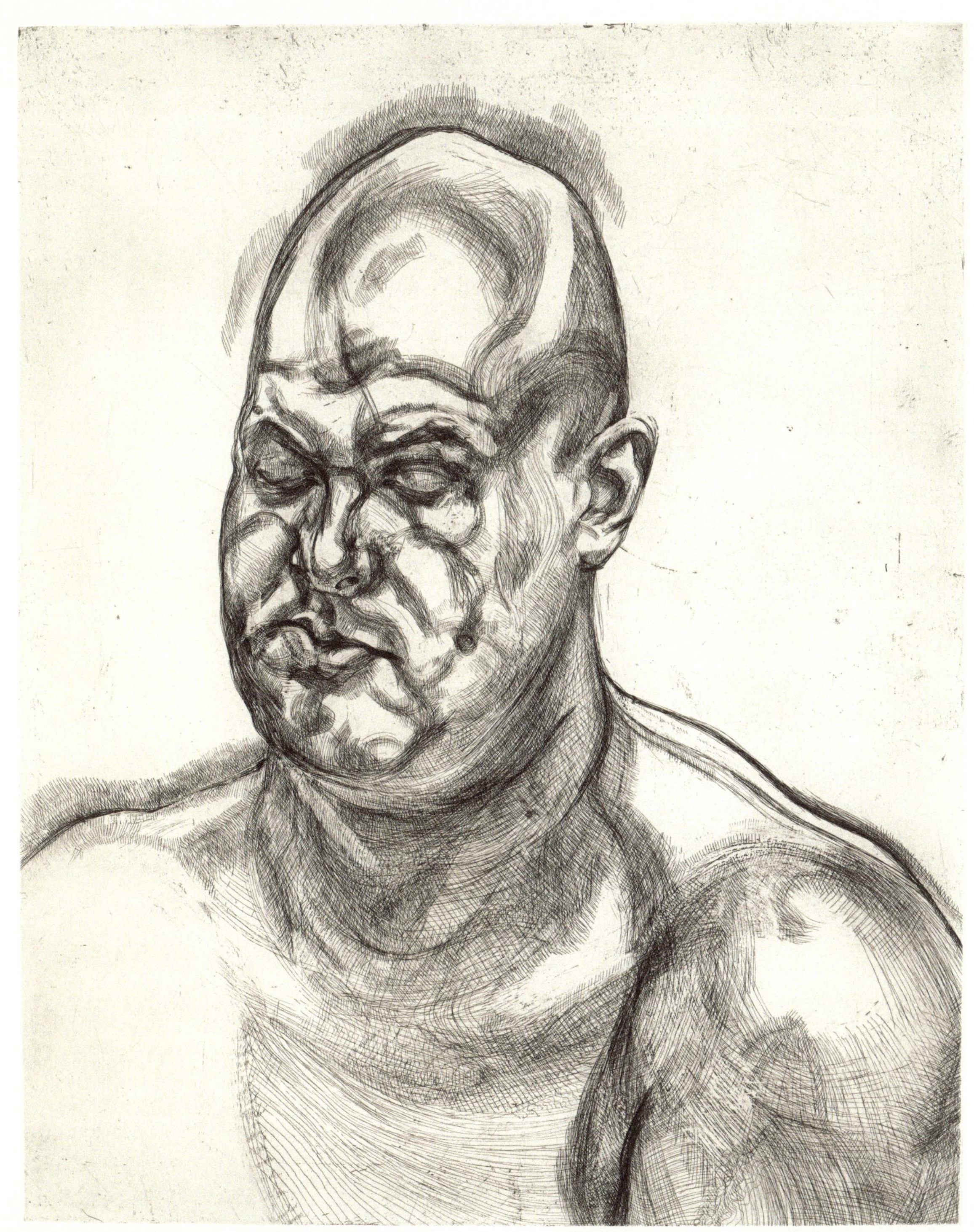

11/40

   Large Sue (Benefits Supervisor Sleeping). 1995. Cat. 50

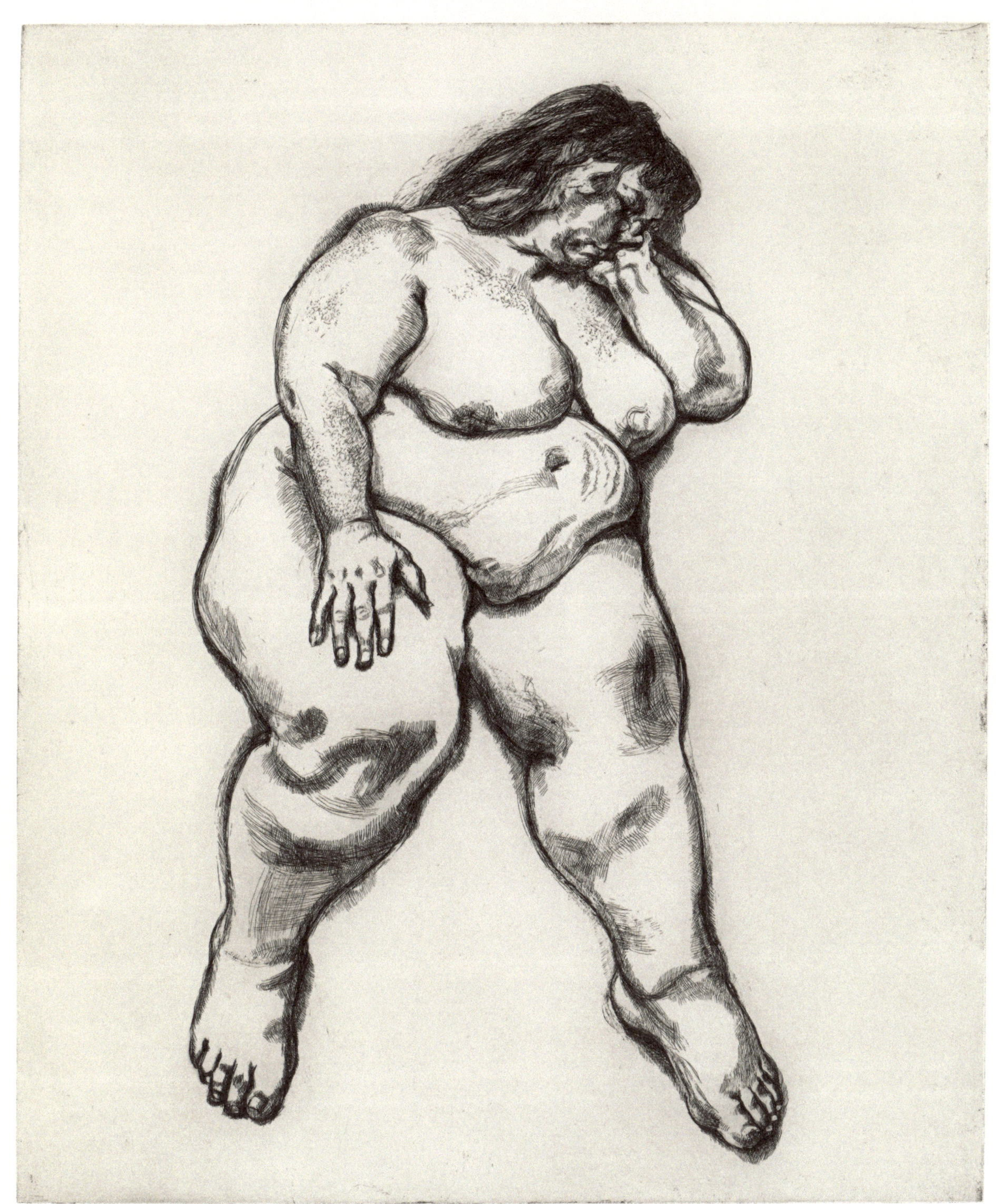
14/36

   Bella in Her Pluto T-Shirt. 1995. Cat. 49

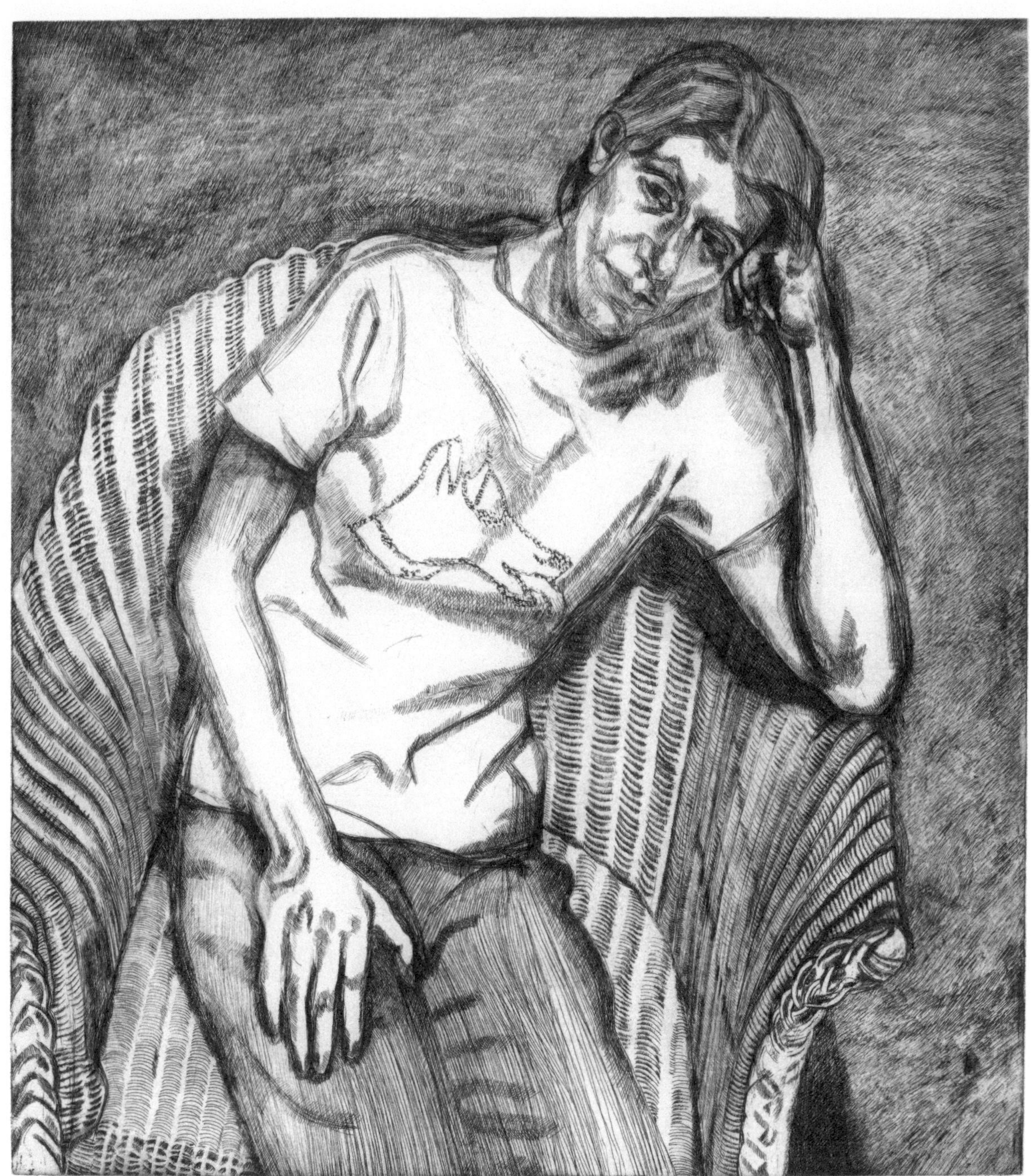

  Self-Portrait: Reflection. 1996. Cat. 51

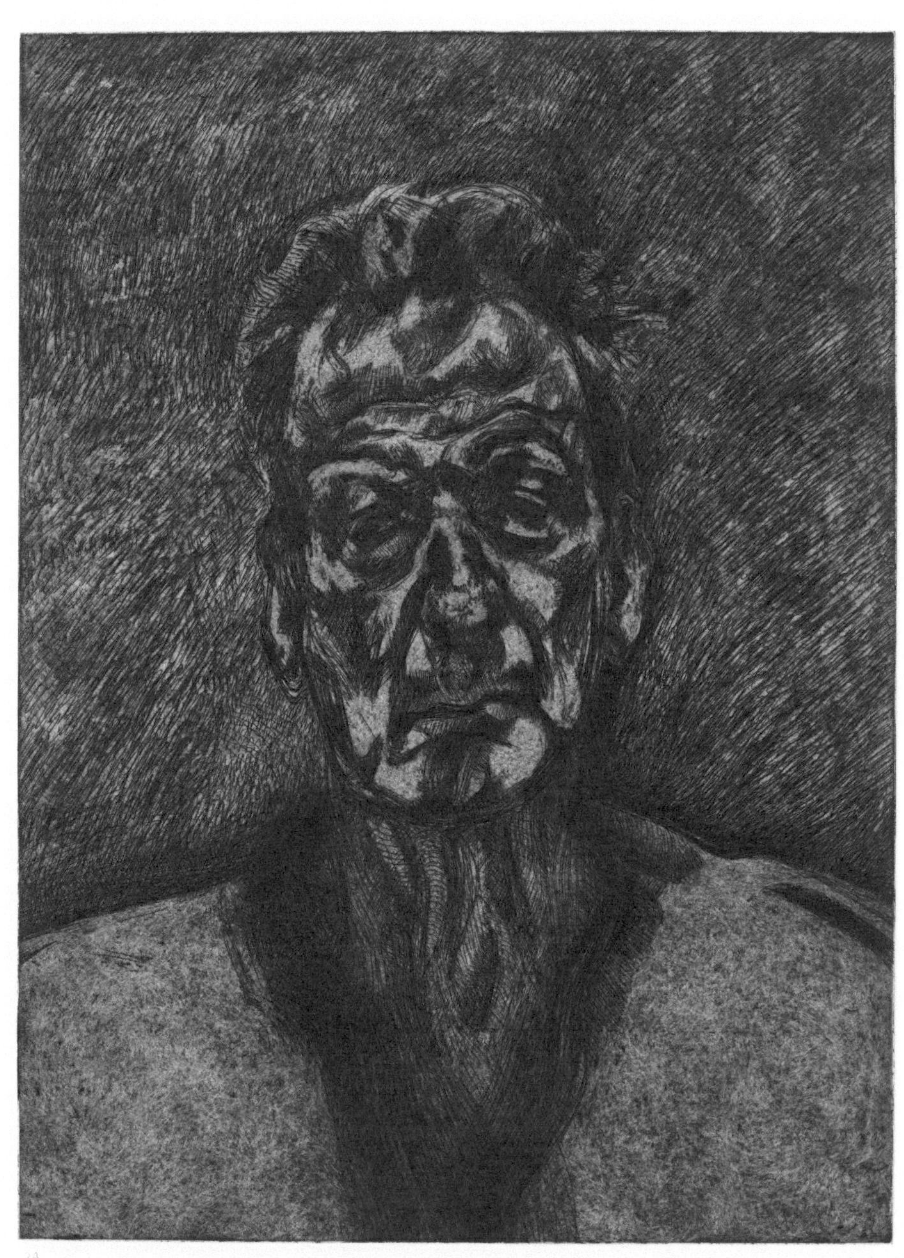

 Susanna. 1996. Cat. 52

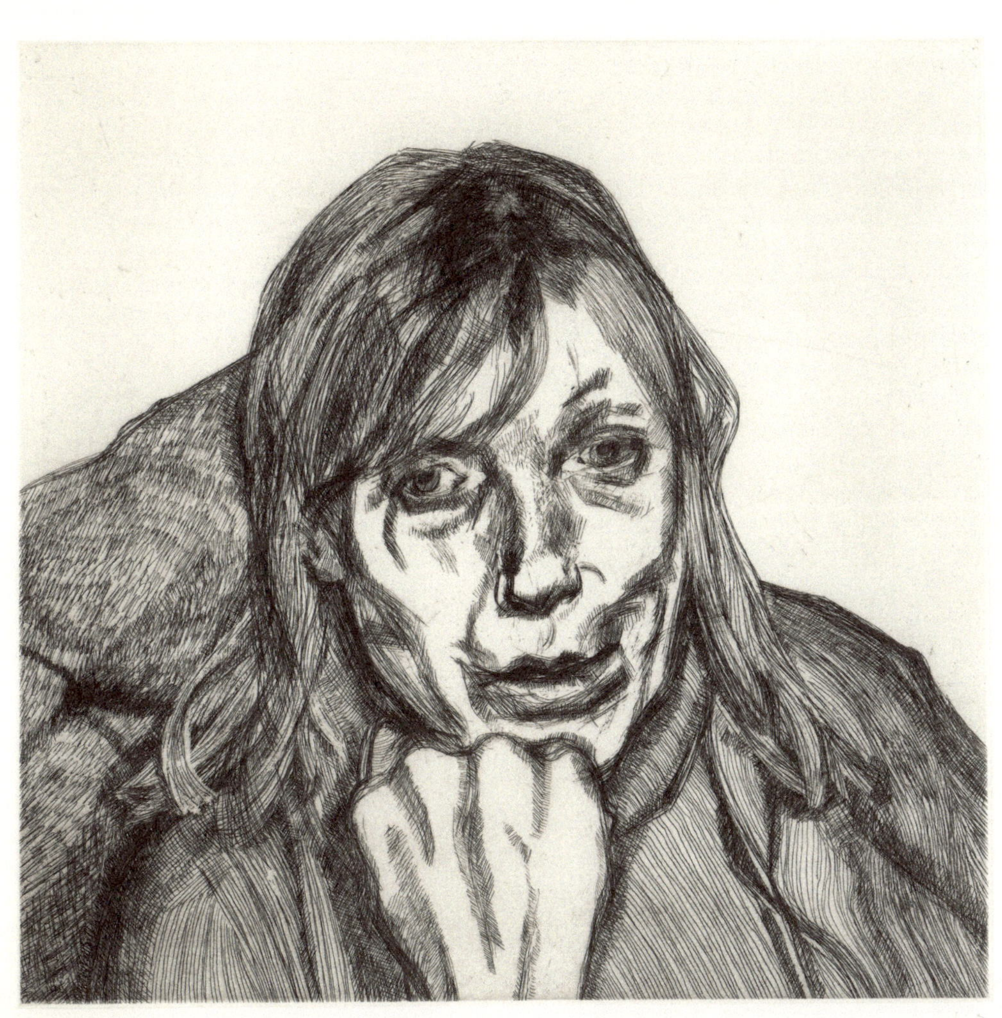

   David Dawson. 1998. Cat. 55

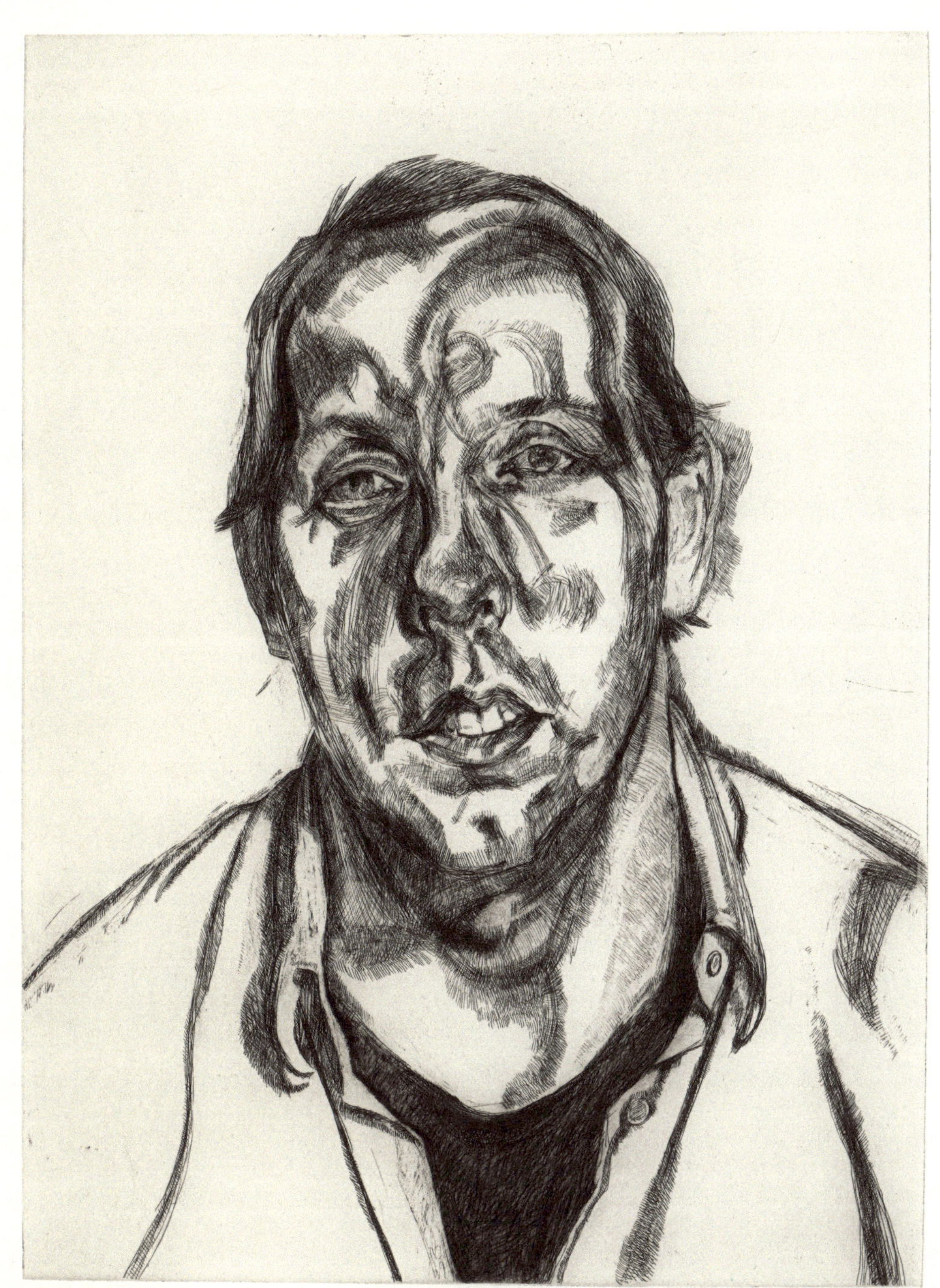

   A Conversation. 1998. Cat. 54

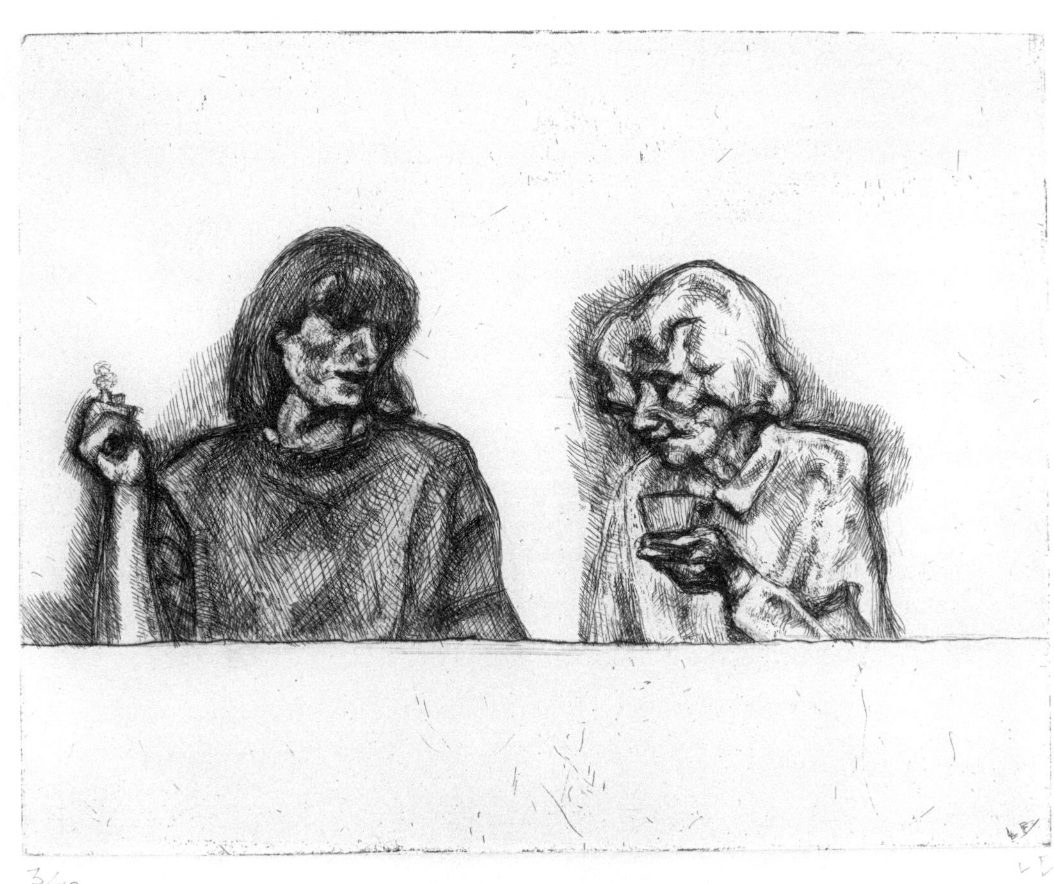

 Garden in Winter. 1999. Cat. 56

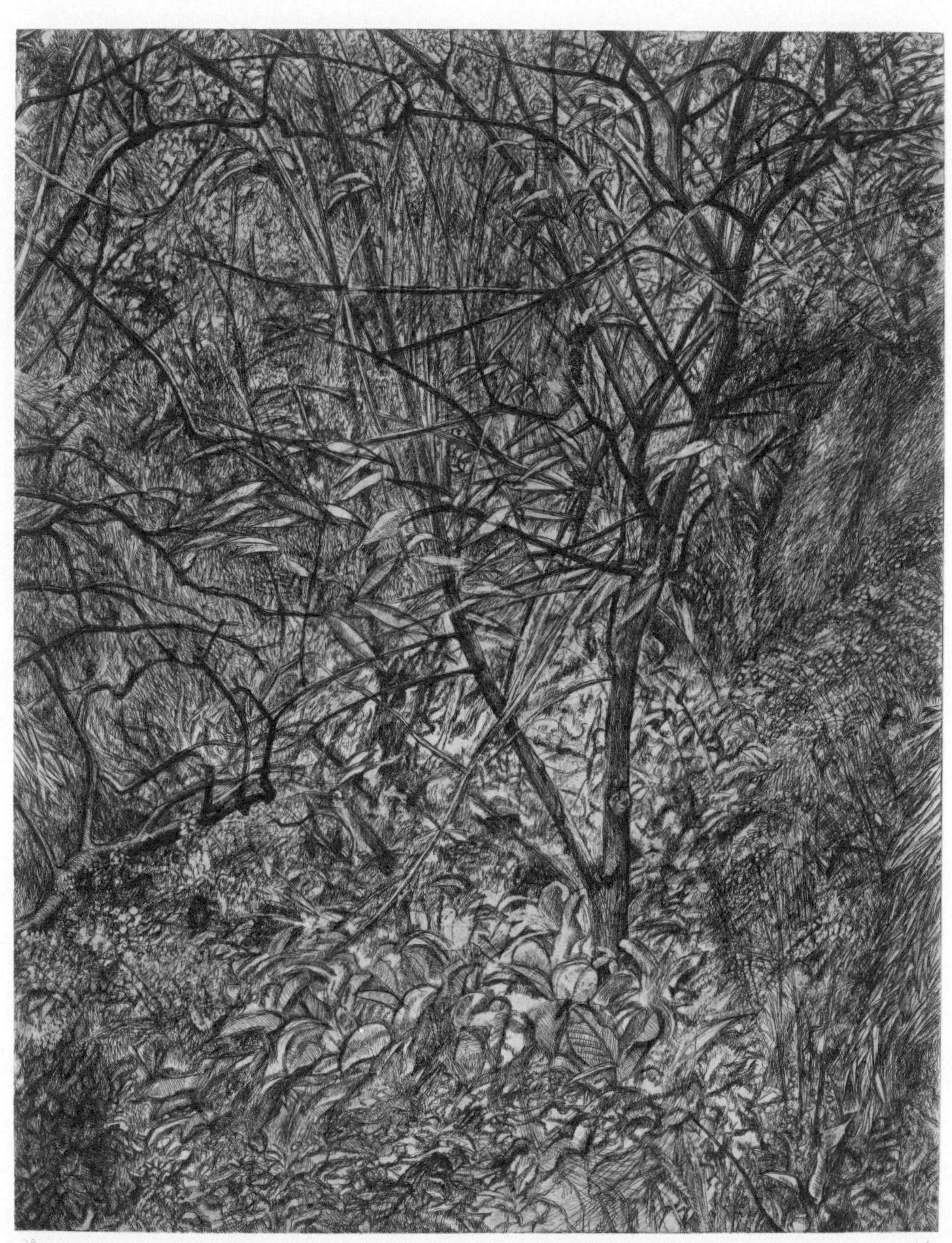

    Head of a Naked Girl. 1999. Cat. 64

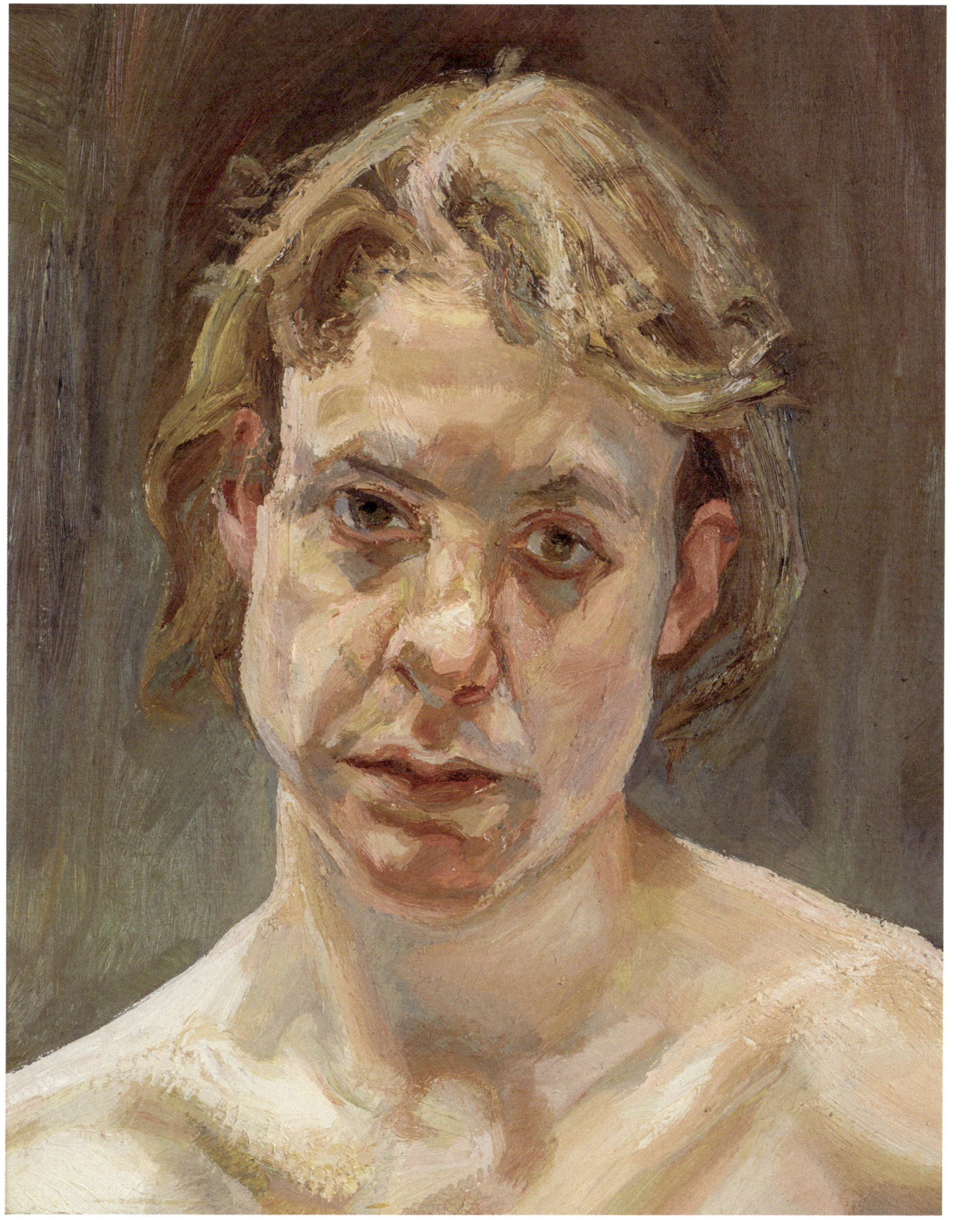

   Head of a Naked Girl. 2000. Cat. 60

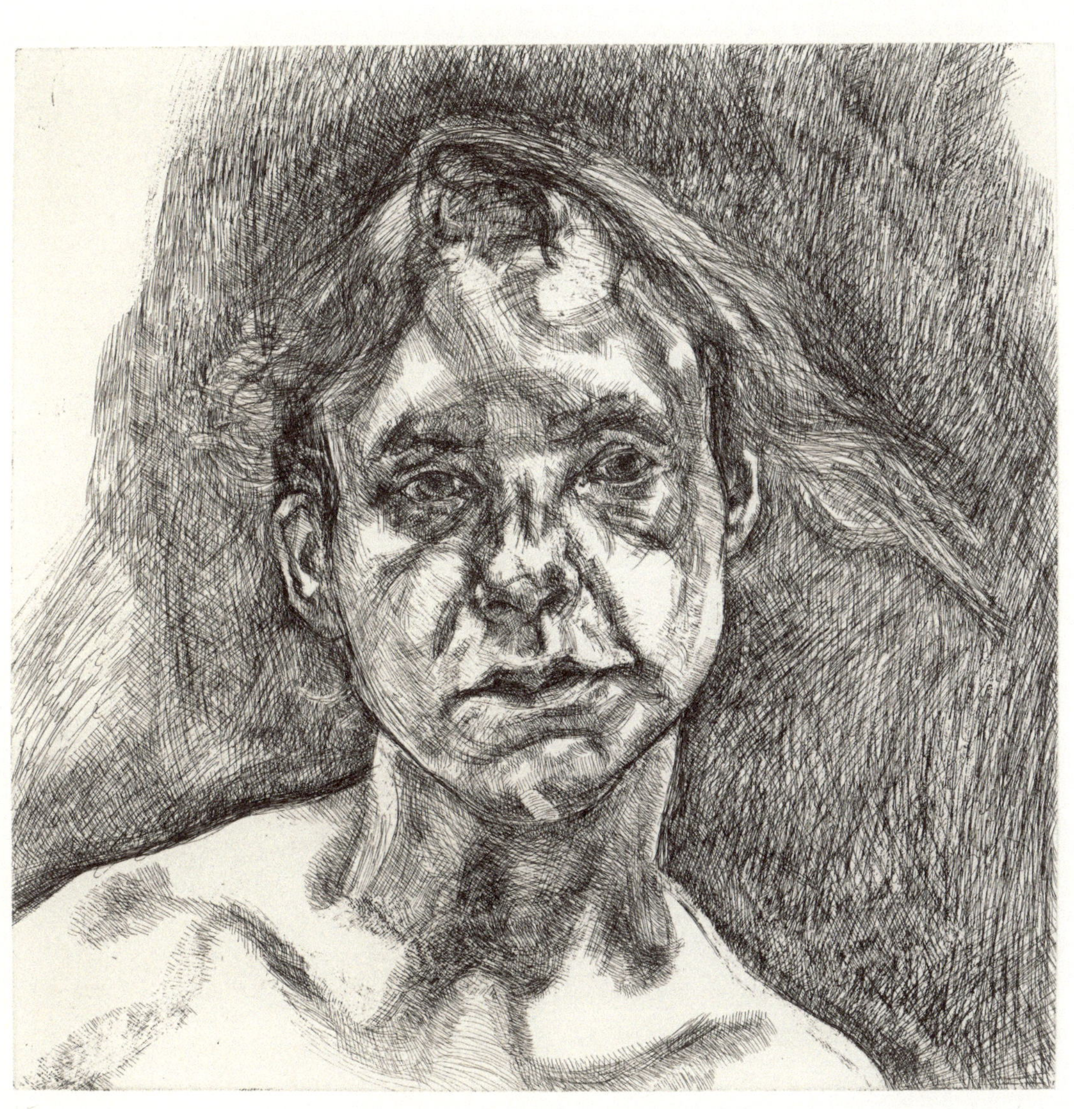

   Head of an Irishman. 1999. Cat. 57

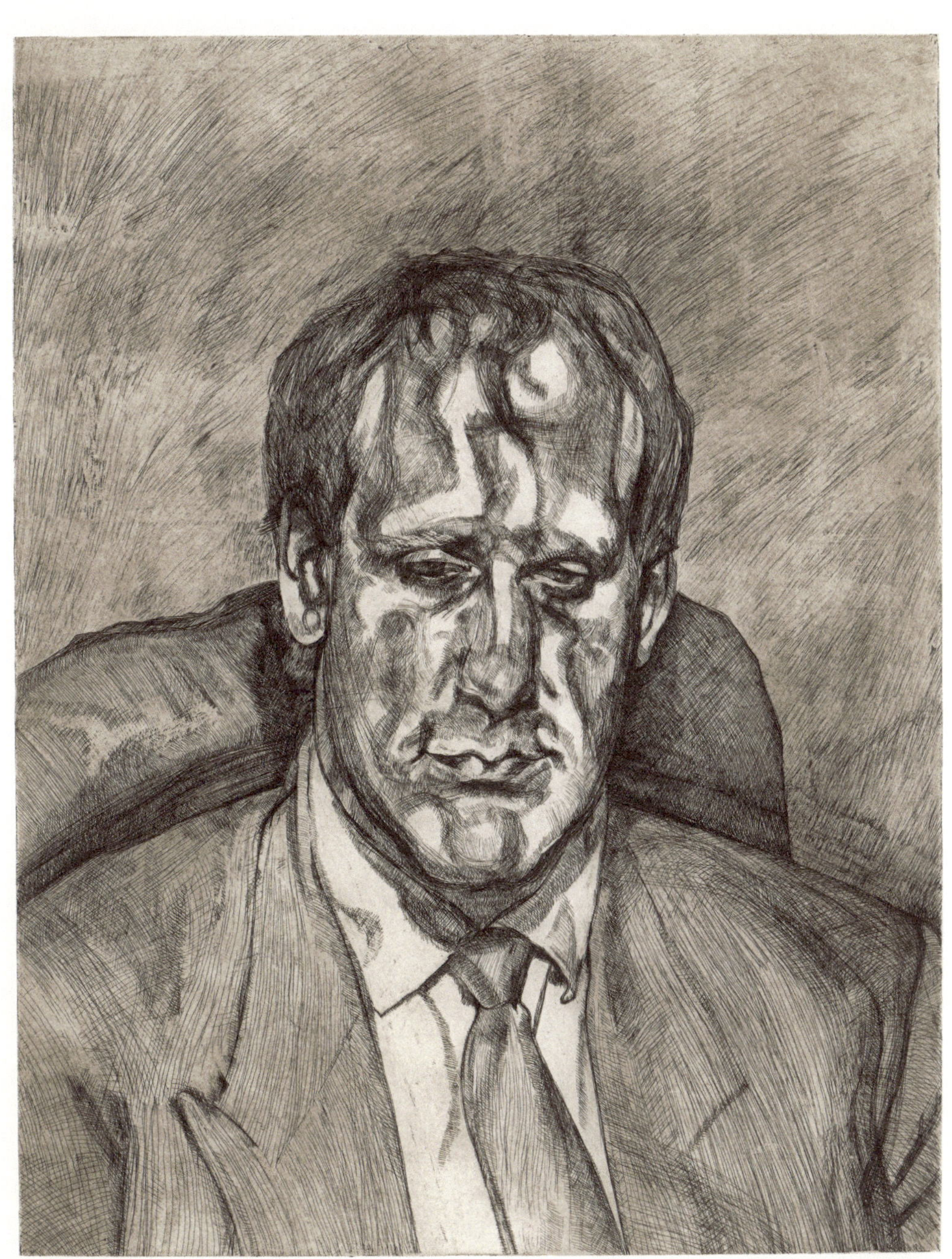

40/46

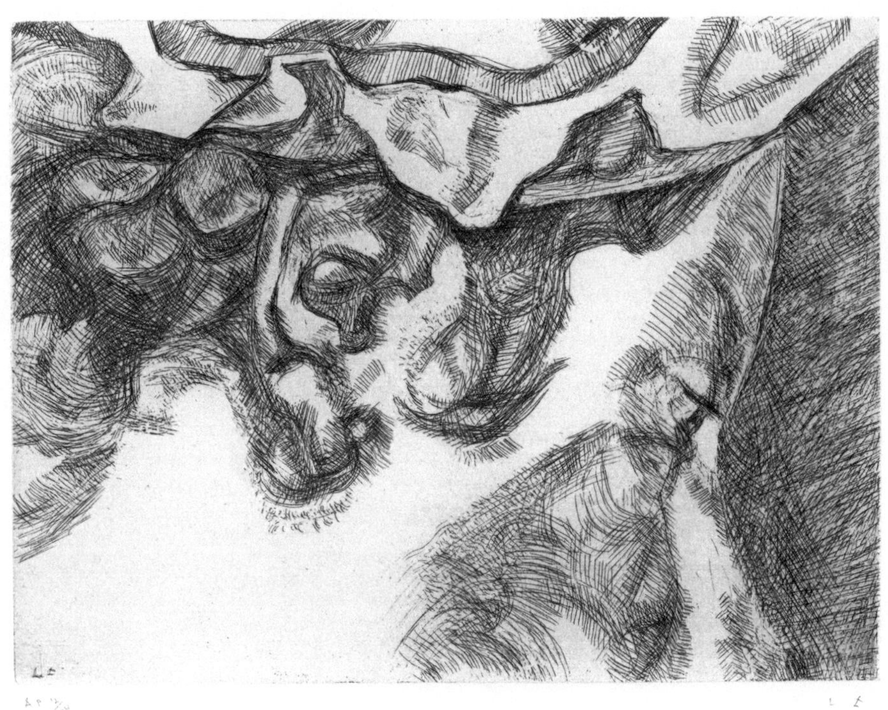

104 *After Chardin* (small plate). 2000. Cat. 59 / *Pluto Aged Twelve*. 2000. Cat. 61

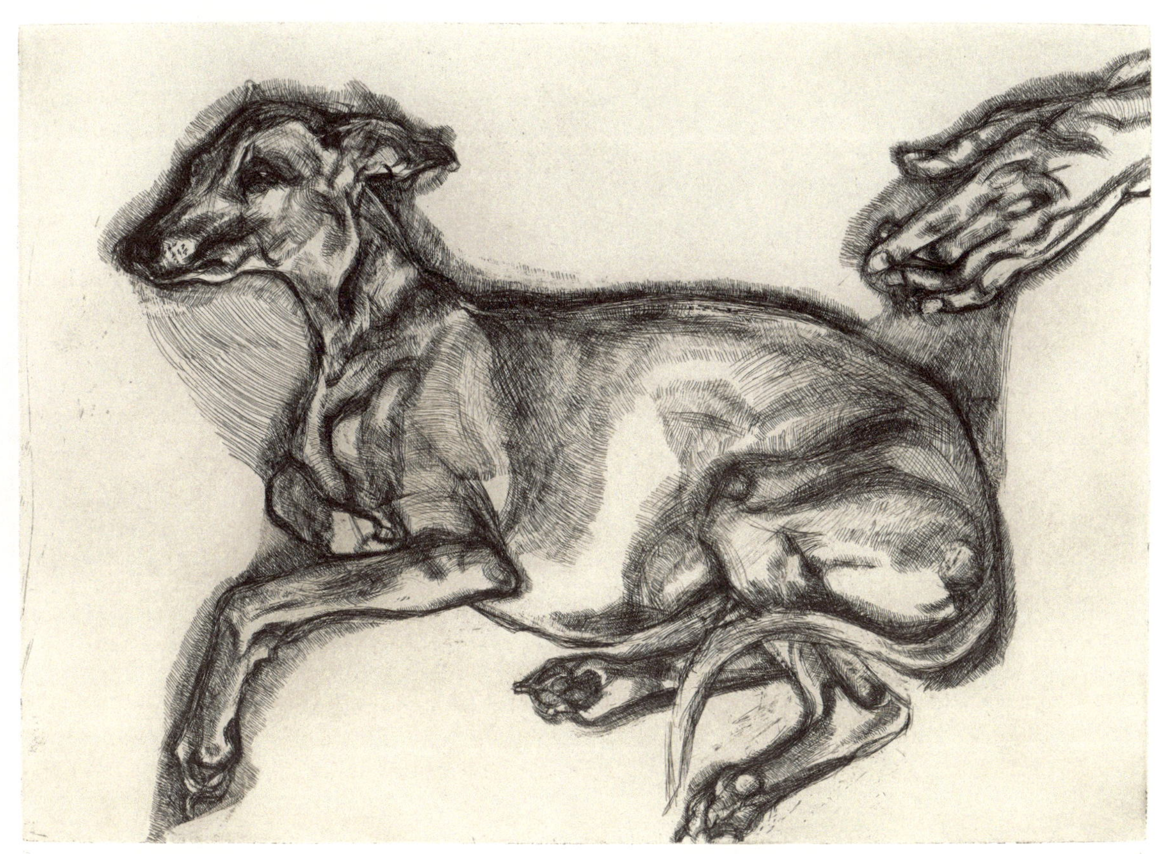

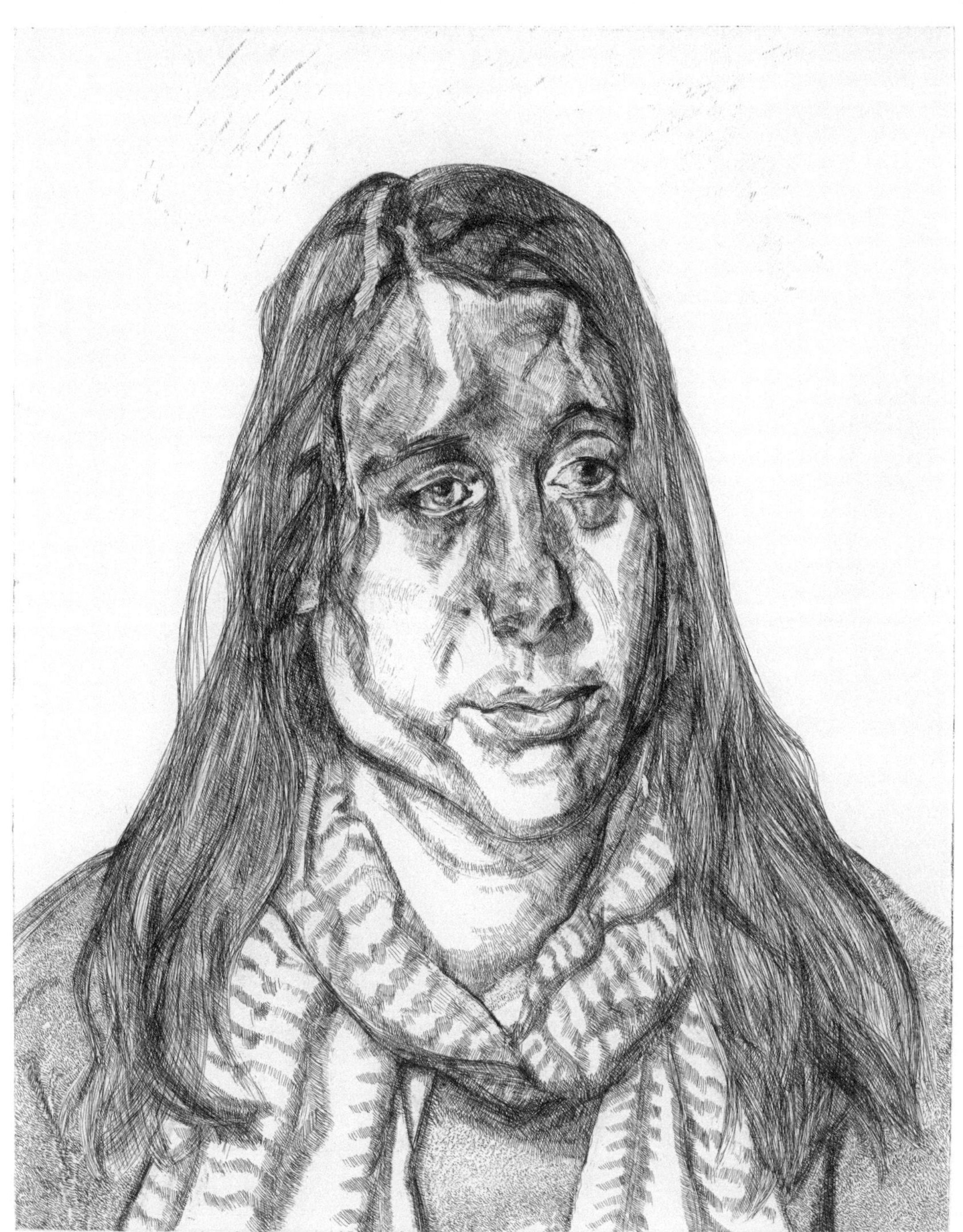

List of works

List of works

All dimensions of work on
paper are sheet sizes

Works on paper:

Cat. 1
Self-Portrait. 1974
Watercolour and graphite on paper
33.3 × 24.1 cm

Cat. 2
A Couple. 1982
Etching. 27.3 × 21 cm

Cat. 3
Bella. 1982
Etching. 56.5 × 53 cm

Cat. 4
Head and Shoulders. 1982
Etching. 38 × 41.5 cm

Cat. 5
Head of Girl I. 1982
Etching. 26.7 × 23.5 cm

Cat. 6
Head of Girl II. 1982
Etching. 34 × 28.3 cm

Cat. 7
Head of a Woman. 1982
Etching. 27.3 × 21 cm

Cat. 8
Head on a Pillow. 1982
Etching. 23 × 24.1 cm

Cat. 9
Lawrence Gowing. 1982
Etching. 33 × 28 cm

Cat. 10
The Painter's Mother. 1982
Etching. 29.5 × 24.2 cm

Cat. 11
The Painter's Mother. 1982
Etching. 41 × 63.5 cm

Cat. 12
Ib. 1984
Etching. 56.5 × 53 cm

Cat. 13
Blond Girl. 1985
Etching. 88 × 71.2 cm

Cat. 14
Girl Holding Her Foot. 1985
Etching. 88 × 71.2 cm

Cat. 15
Head of Bruce Bernard. 1985
Etching. 51 × 47 cm

Cat. 16
Man Posing. 1985
Etching. 87.5 × 73.6 cm

Cat. 17
Thistle. 1985
Etching. 31 × 25 cm

Cat. 18
Bella. 1987
Etching. 69.3 × 56.5 cm

Cat. 19
Girl Sitting. 1987
Etching. 61 × 77.5 cm

Cat. 20
Head of a Man. 1987
Etching. 51.2 × 45 cm

Cat. 21
*Lord Goodman in His Yellow
Pyjamas*. 1987
Etching. 48.2 × 55.6 cm

Cat. 22
Naked Man on a Bed. 1987
Etching. 57.2 × 76.2 cm

Cat. 23
Head of Ib. 1988
Etching. 36.2 × 28 cm

Cat. 24
Man Resting. 1988
Etching. 47 × 50.2 cm

Cat. 25
Pluto. 1988
Etching. 42 × 68.6 cm

Cat. 26
Cerith. 1989
Pastel over etching on paper
34.9 × 26 cm

Cat. 27
Two Men in the Studio. 1989
Etching. 40.7 × 36.2 cm

Cat. 28
Head and Shoulders of a Girl. 1990
Etching. 78 × 63.5 cm

Cat. 29
Naked Man on a Bed. 1990
Etching. 58.5 × 57.2 cm

Cat. 30
Esther. 1991
Etching. 44 × 39.3 cm

Cat. 31
Four Figures. 1991
Etching. 68.5 × 94.5 cm

Cat. 32
Kai. 1991-92
Etching. 79 × 62.2 cm

Cat. 33
Woman on a Bed. 1991-92
Etching. 44.4 × 39.3 cm

Cat. 34
Head of a Man. 1992
Etching. 42 × 40 cm

Cat. 35
Landscape. 1993
Etching. 34.5 × 38.7 cm

Cat. 36
Large Head. 1993
Etching. 78.8 × 63.5 cm

Cat. 37
The Egyptian Book. 1994
Etching. 46.3 × 42.5 cm

Cat. 38
Reclining Figure. 1994
Etching with drypoint. 26.7 × 33 cm
Working proof of the first state
of three.

Cat. 39
Reclining Figure. 1994
Etching with drypoint. 26 × 33 cm
Working proof of the first state,
with pastel additions by the artist
requesting the erasure of a section
of the composition.

Cat. 40
Reclining Figure, 1994
Etching with drypoint. 26.5 × 33 cm
Working proof, between the first
and second states, with a section
of the composition erased.

Cat. 41
Reclining Figure. 1994
Etching with drypoint. 30.6 × 38.4 cm
Working proof, between the first
and second states, with new work
by the artist in the erased areas.

Cat. 42
Reclining Figure. 1994
Etching with drypoint. 26.8 × 33.2 cm
Working proof of the second state
of three.

Cat. 43
Reclining Figure. 1994
Etching with drypoint. 27 × 33.3 cm
Working proof of the second state,
with pastel additions by the artist
requesting the erasure of a section
of the composition.

Cat. 44
Reclining Figure. 1994
Etching with drypoint. 30.7 × 39.2 cm
Working proof, between the second
and third states, with a section of
the composition erased.

Cat. 45
Reclining Figure. 1994
Etching with drypoint. 29.6 × 38.4 cm
Proof of the third (final) state, before
the edition of thirty in this state
(there were no editions of the first
two states).

Cat. 46
Reclining Figure. 1994
Etching with drypoint. 26.6 × 33 cm
Proof of the third (final) state, on
off-white paper, before the edition
of thirty in this state (there were no
editions of the first two states).

Cat. 47
Reclining Figure. 1994
Etching with drypoint. 23.8 × 34.9 cm
Impression from the cancelled plate.

Cat. 48
Reclining Figure. 1994
Etching. 32.3 × 42 cm

Cat. 49
Bella in Her Pluto T-Shirt. 1995
Etching. 82 × 72.5 cm

Cat. 50
*Large Sue (Benefits Supervisor
Sleeping)*. 1995
Etching. 82.5 × 67.3 cm

Cat. 51
Self-Portrait: Reflection. 1996
Etching. 87.5 × 70 cm

Cat. 52
Susanna. 1996
Etching. 50.2 × 49.8 cm

Cat. 53
Woman with an Arm Tattoo. 1996
Etching. 70 × 91.5 cm

Cat. 54
A Conversation. 1998
Etching. 33.3 × 38 cm

Cat. 55
David Dawson. 1998
Etching. 75.7 × 57.2 cm

Cat. 56
Garden in Winter. 1999
Etching. 98.5 × 76.3 cm

Cat. 57
Head of an Irishman. 1999
Etching. 97.2 × 78.1 cm

Cat. 58
After Chardin (large plate). 2000
Etching. 94.3 × 76.8 cm

Cat. 59
After Chardin (small plate). 2000
Etching. 37.5 × 50.8 cm

Cat. 60
Head of a Naked Girl. 2000
Etching. 58.8 × 57 cm

Cat. 61
Pluto Aged Twelve. 2000
Etching. 57.1 × 72.3 cm

Cat. 62
Portrait Head. 2001
Etching. 76.2 × 57.1 cm

Paintings:

Cat. 63
Double Portrait. 1988-90
Oil on canvas. 113.3 × 134.6 cm

Cat. 64
Head of a Naked Girl. 1999
Oil on canvas. 51.4 × 40.6 cm

LUCIAN FREUD – A CLOSER LOOK
Works from the UBS Art Collection

© 2015 Louisiana Museum of Modern Art
and the contributors

Edited by Michael Juul Holm, Anders Kold
and Stephen McCoubrey
Desk Editor Sidsel Kjærulff Rasmussen
Design Michael Jensen
Translations from the Danish by James Manley
Produced for Louisiana Museum of Modern Art
by Strandberg Publishing
Printed by Narayana Press
Printed in Denmark 2015
ISBN 978-87-92877-43-7

All works © The Lucian Freud Archive 2015
Photos: Courtesy of the Lucian Freud Archive /
Bridgeman Images, except cat. 38-47:
Photo by Todd White. Courtesy Blain|Southern and p. 14:
Ill in Paris. 1948. Etching on wove paper. 25 × 32.6 cm.
Christie's Images Limited. © 2015 Christie's Images,
London/Scala, Florence

This catalogue is published on the occasion of the exhibition

Louisiana on Paper
LUCIAN FREUD – A CLOSER LOOK
Louisiana Museum of Modern Art
3 September – 29 November 2015

Curator Anders Kold
Curatorial Coordinator Arne Schmidt-Petersen
Exhibition Producer and Conservator Jesper Lund Madsen
Graphic Designers Marie d'Origny Lübecker
and Nina Krogh Christensen

www.louisiana.dk

With support from:

Louisiana's Main Corporate Partners:

REPUBLIC OF **Fritz Hansen**®

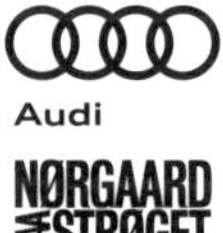

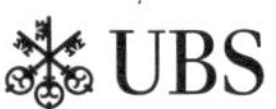

Sponsor of Louisiana Learning:

🔑 UBS